KT-563-493

Published by:

Wiley Publishing, Inc.

111 River St.
Hoboken, NJ 07030-5774

ISBN 978-0-470-38438-1

Editor: Marc Nadeau
Production Editor: Michael Brumitt
Photo Editor: Richard Fox
Cartographer: Liz Puhl
Production by Wiley Indianapolis Composition Services

For information on our other products and services or to obtain technical
support, please contact our Customer Care Department within the U.S.
at 800/762-2974, outside the U.S. at 317/572-3993 or fax 317/572-4002.

Wiley also publishes its books in a variety of electronic formats. Some
content that appears in print may not be available in electronic formats.

Manufactured in China

5   4   3   2

Frommer's®

Amsterdam
day BY day™
2nd Edition

by George McDonald

Wiley Publishing, Inc.

Contents

A Note from the Editorial Director

Organizing your time. That's what this guide is all about.

Other guides give you long lists of things to see and do and then expect you to fit the pieces together. The Day by Day guides are different. These guides tell you the best of everything, and then they show you how to see it *in the smartest, most time-efficient way*. Our authors have designed detailed itineraries organized by time, neighborhood, or special interest. And each tour comes with a bulleted map that takes you from stop to stop.

Hoping to admire some van Goghs, or buy some tulip bulbs to take home? Planning to pedal along some canals, or take a whirlwind tour of the very best that Amsterdam has to offer? Whatever your interest or schedule, the Day by Days give you the smartest routes to follow. Not only do we take you to the top attractions, hotels, and restaurants, but we also help you access those special moments that locals get to experience—those "finds" that turn tourists into travelers.

The Day by Days are also your top choice if you're looking for one complete guide for all your travel needs. The best hotels and restaurants for every budget, the greatest shopping values, the wildest nightlife—it's all here.

Why should you trust our judgment? Because our authors personally visit each place they write about. They're an independent lot who say what they think and would never include places they wouldn't recommend to their best friends. They're also open to suggestions from readers. If you'd like to contact them, please send your comments our way at feedback@frommers.com, and we'll pass them on.

Enjoy your Day by Day guide—the most helpful travel companion you can buy. And have the trip of a lifetime.

Warm regards,

Kelly Regan

Kelly Regan, Editorial Director
Frommer's Travel Guides

About the Author

George McDonald has lived and worked in Amsterdam as deputy editor of KLM's in-flight magazine, *Holland Herald*. Now a freelance journalist and travel writer, he has written extensively about Amsterdam and the Netherlands for magazines and travel books, including *Frommer's Amsterdam; Frommer's Belgium, Holland & Luxembourg; Frommer's Europe;* and *Europe For Dummies.*

Acknowledgments

The Frommer's Editorial Team would like to acknowledge the hard work and convivial spirit of our much-admired writer, the late Haas Mroue. Haas was a perennial contributor to a range of Frommer's titles, from *Paris From $95 a Day* to the first edition of *Amsterdam Day by Day.* A consummate professional, Haas was always a joy to work with, peppering his correspondence with such nuggets as to make even travel editors jealous of his sophisticated globetrotting lifestyle. We give him heartfelt thanks for his contributions to our books and for brightening our days with his genial spirit. He was truly one of a kind and is sorely missed.

An Additional Note

Please be advised that travel information is subject to change at any time—and this is especially true of prices. We therefore suggest that you write or call ahead for confirmation when making your travel plans. The authors, editors, and publisher cannot be held responsible for the experiences of readers while traveling. Your safety is important to us, however, so we encourage you to stay alert and be aware of your surroundings.

Star Ratings, Icons & Abbreviations

Every hotel, restaurant, and attraction listing in this guide has been ranked for quality, value, service, amenities, and special features using a **star-rating system.** Hotels, restaurants, attractions, shopping, and nightlife are rated on a scale of zero stars (recommended) to three stars (exceptional). In addition to the star-rating system, we also use a **kids** icon to point out the best bets for families. Within each tour, we recommend cafes, bars, or restaurants where you can take a break. Each of these stops appears in a shaded box marked with a coffee-cup-shaped bullet ☕.

The following **abbreviations** are used for credit cards:

| AE | American Express | DISC | Discover | V | Visa |
| DC | Diners Club | MC | MasterCard | | |

Frommers.com

Now that you have this guidebook to help you plan a great trip, visit our website at **www.frommers.com** for additional travel information on more than 4,000 destinations. We update features regularly to give you instant access to the most current trip-planning information available. At Frommers.com, you'll find scoops on the best airfares, lodging rates, and car rental bargains. You can even book your travel online through our reliable travel booking partners. Other popular features include:

- Online updates of our most popular guidebooks
- Vacation sweepstakes and contest giveaways
- Newsletters highlighting the hottest travel trends
- Podcasts, interactive maps, and up-to-the-minute events listings
- Opinionated blog entries by Arthur Frommer himself
- Online travel message boards with featured travel discussions

A Note on Prices

In the "Take a Break" and "Best Bets" sections of this book, we have used a system of dollar signs to show a range of costs for 1 night in a hotel (the price of a double-occupancy room) or the cost of an entree at a restaurant. Use the following table to decipher the dollar signs:

Cost	Hotels	Restaurants
$	under $100	under $10
$$	$100–$200	$10–$20
$$$	$200–$300	$20–$30
$$$$	$300–$400	$30–$40
$$$$$	over $400	over $40

An Invitation to the Reader

In researching this book, we discovered many wonderful places—hotels, restaurants, shops, and more. We're sure you'll find others. Please tell us about them, so we can share the information with your fellow travelers in upcoming editions. If you were disappointed with a recommendation, we'd love to know that, too. Please write to:

Frommer's Amsterdam Day by Day, 2nd Edition
Wiley Publishing, Inc. • 111 River St. • Hoboken, NJ 07030-5774

13 Favorite
Moments

13 Favorite **Moments**

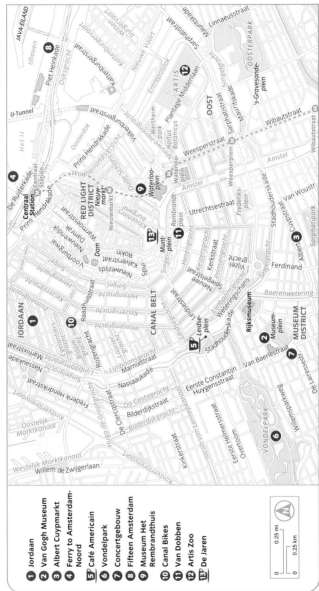

Previous page: A classic Amsterdam canal vista.

So many of my favorite moments in Amsterdam are outdoors. Even in midwinter this city bustles with an infectious energy on its narrow streets, long canals, and many humpbacked bridges. Whichever time you choose to visit, you'll be struck, I'm sure, by how lively and bright this city really is. Here are some of my favorite moments, both outdoors and indoors, that have placed Amsterdam so close to my heart.

1 **Strolling in the Jordaan.** The first thing I do after arriving in Amsterdam—whether I'm here in the dead of winter or the brilliance of summer—is to take a long stroll in the Jordaan up and down its beautiful tree-fringed canals. I like to look at the buildings and the houseboats and then stop for a strong coffee at a neighborhood cafe. Then I'm ready for my first day in this vibrant and architecturally rich city. *See p 15.*

2 **Admiring the paintings at the Van Gogh Museum,** late in the afternoon just before the museum closes, is one of the highlights of a trip to Amsterdam. That's when the usually crowded second-floor gallery is almost empty and I can stand there, lost in my own world, admiring Vincent's brush strokes without being shoved around by the throngs. *See p 7.*

3 **Picking out fruit at the Albert Cuyp Market,** early in the morning (between 8–9am) as the many outdoor stands on this long street are being prepared for a day of shoppers, is a quintessential Amsterdam

A flower stand at the Albert Cuyp Market.

You can see Sunflowers *and many other famous works at the Van Gogh Museum.*

moment. I like to watch the fresh fish being laid out on ice, imagining how, not long ago, they were swimming in the North Sea. *See p 76.*

4 **Catching the ferry to Amsterdam-Noord (North),** from behind Centraal Station, immediately gives me a sense of space. The narrow IJ channel is full of boats, ferries, and barges, and I ride the free ferry to the north bank and back, just to take in the views. *See p 161.*

5 **Living the Americain Dream,** by taking coffee in the Art Deco ambience of the Amsterdam American Hotel's Café Americain. Visitors will be pleased to learn that the service has improved considerably since a postwar Dutch writer dubbed the waiters here "unemployed knife throwers." *See p 85.*

You can get a whole new perspective on Amsterdam from a canal bike.

6 Strolling in Vondelpark on a sunny afternoon makes me feel as if I'm a million miles from any city. The English-style park is an echo of the countryside translated to the city, and when I'm lucky, I can stop and smell the roses, which bloom in late summer. *See p 78.*

7 An evening at the Concertgebouw, an acoustically perfect concert hall that many top conductors and orchestras visit, is one of my favorite ways to spend an evening in Amsterdam. *See p 116.*

8 Watching the hectic choreography of the gorgeous waitstaff as they serve their trendy clientele at Jamie Oliver's restaurant Fifteen Amsterdam is mesmerizing. If you fail to make reservations, just sit at the bar and order appetizers (it's cheaper, anyway) as you take in the heady atmosphere of the young chefs in action in the open kitchen. *See p 97.*

9 Standing alone in Rembrandt's bedroom over 500 years after he last slept there fills me with awe. This is where he rested after a long day at the canvas, I think to myself over and over again. Come early in the day or right at closing time and you'll have a good chance at being alone too. *See p 97.*

10 Peeking at houseboats at eye-level as I pedal a canal bike lets me see Amsterdam from a different angle. The Jordaan canals are especially dense with lived-in houseboats. *See p 15.*

11 Eating a raw-herring sandwich with pickles and onions with the locals at Van Dobben is what I do on my first day in Amsterdam. Somehow, the taste of the North Sea helps whet my appetite for all that's to come. *See p 96.*

12 A morning at the zoo makes me feel like a kid again. I walk to Artis Zoo, in the Plantage district east of the center city, to watch the animals being fed—a minisafari in the city. *See p 34.*

13 A frothy Grolsch beer at a waterside cafe at dusk is my favorite ending to any day in Amsterdam. I like to sit outside on the waterside terrace at De Jaren on Nieuwe Doelenstraat and stretch my legs, watching the boats passing by on the Binnenamstel. *See p 106.*

Vondelpark is the perfect place to relax on a sunny day.

The Best in **One Day**

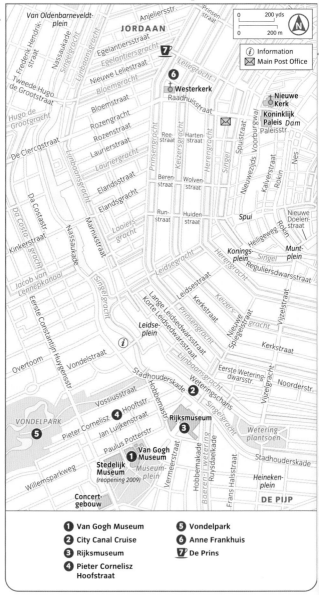

Legend:
- (i) Information
- ✉ Main Post Office

Numbered sites:
1. Van Gogh Museum
2. City Canal Cruise
3. Rijksmuseum
4. Pieter Cornelisz Hoofstraat
5. Vondelpark
6. Anne Frankhuis
7. De Prins

Previous page: Tulips at a city market.

A msterdam is a compact city, so this 1-day tour allows you to see the major highlights with minimal time spent on public transportation. Wear comfortable shoes and be sure to look both ways as you cross major intersections—bicyclists follow no rules here and they travel at alarming speeds. START: Tram 2 or 5 to Museumplein.

1 ★★★ **Van Gogh Museum.** This gem of a museum houses the world's largest collection of Vincent van Gogh's work: 200 paintings, 580 drawings, and over 700 letters by Vincent himself (most written to his brother, Theo). A four-story building designed by Gerrit Rietveld houses the permanent collection. Although most of the work here is by van Gogh, the third floor includes paintings by Impressionist artists such as Monet, Seurat, Pissarro, Gauguin, and Toulouse-Lautrec. An adjacent building in the shape of an ellipse, designed by Japanese "organic" architect Kisho Kurokawa and opened in 1999, houses temporary exhibits. These change every 3 or 4 months and often include some of van Gogh's drawings. Check the museum website for the schedule. ⏱ *3 hr. Arrive at 9:45am to beat the crowds; buy tickets from the museum's website to* *cut down on wait time. Paulus Potterstraat 7 (at Museumplein).* ☎ *020/ 570-5200. www.vangoghmuseum.nl. Admission 13€ adults, 2.50€ kids 13–17. Sat–Thurs 10am–6pm; Fri 10am–10pm. Closed Jan 1. Tram: 2, 3, 5, or 12 to Van Baerlestraat.*

2 ★★ **City Canal Cruise.** There's no better way to discover Amsterdam than from its canals. Sure, it's touristy, but I can't think of a better way to see a large chunk of Amsterdam in a short time. You can opt to sit outside (on some boats) if the weather permits or settle into a comfortable seat indoors. A typical cruise, for instance with the Blue Boat Company, has the boat loop northward on the western canals, circle Centraal Station, and loop back to the departure point along the eastern canals. There's commentary in English, so you'll know

A man studies one of van Gogh's self-portraits.

Touring Amsterdam by canal boat can help you get a feel for the city.

what you're seeing. ⏱ *1½ hr. Stadhouderskade (at Leideseplein).* ☎ *020/679-1370. www.canalcruises.nl. Tickets 9€ adults; 6€ kids 4–12 (prices may vary slightly from line to line). Departures every 30 min. 10am–6pm Apr–Sept; every hr. 10am–6pm Oct–Mar. Tram: 1, 2, 5, 7, or 10 to Leidseplein.*

③ ★★★ Rijksmuseum. Petrus Josephus Hubertus Cuypers (1827–1921), the "grandfather of modern Dutch architecture," designed this museum in a monumental Dutch neo-Renaissance style. Cuypers, a Catholic, slipped in more than a dab of neo-Gothic, too, causing the country's thoroughly Protestant King William III to scorn what he called "that cathedral." The building opened in 1885 to a less-than-enthusiastic public reception. Most of the museum is closed for major renovations until 2010 at the earliest, but a small section of the museum, the Philips Wing, remains open throughout the renovation to showcase "the Masterpieces"—the museum's highlights. Rembrandt and Vermeer lovers, don't panic: You can still see *Nightwatch* and *The Kitchen Maid*. In fact, you'll find an entire room filled with Rembrandts. Three other galleries are dedicated to Vermeer, Frans Hals, and Jan Steen. ⏱ *1½ hr. Jan Luijkenstraat 1 (at Museumplein).*

Van Gogh: 10 Years of Genius

The second floor of the Van Gogh Museum's permanent exhibit gives you a fascinating chronological insight into van Gogh's life and work. Although his career as a painter lasted only 10 years—during which time he completed over 900 paintings—you'll see stunning shifts in style and color as you move from one year and one geographical area to another. For example, compare the dark and somber *Potato Eaters* from his earliest work in Holland in 1885 to the light and airy *View of the Roofs of Paris*, completed just a year later.

The paintings van Gogh completed in Arles—like his famous *Bedroom at Arles* (1888)—explode with color. There are several lesser-known paintings from the last year of his life, including the ominous *Wheatfield Under Thundercloud*, painted shortly before his suicide in 1890.

☎ 020/674-7000. www.rijksmuseum. nl. Admission 10€ adults, free for kids under 19. Sat–Thurs 9am–6pm; Fri 9am–8:30pm. Closed Jan. 1. Tram: 2 or 5 to Hobbemastraat.

④ ★ Pieter Cornelisz Hooft-straat. The city's most upscale shopping district lies just a block from the Rijksmuseum, so those with shopping aspirations should take advantage of the opportunity to spend an hour strolling the short but oh-so-chic P.C. Hooftstraat (locals usually shorten the name to "P.C. Hooft"). You'll find the quintessential jet-set boutiques such as Louis Vuitton, Armani, Dolce & Gabbana, Ralph Lauren, and Gucci clustered on this primo stretch of real estate. ⏱ *30–60 min. Shops open Mon–Sat 10am–6pm. Tram: 2 or 5 to Hobbemastraat.*

⑤ ★★ Vondelpark. A 2-minute stroll from the Rijksmuseum and P.C. Hooftstraat brings you to the largest and most popular park in Amsterdam. Vondelpark is 44 hectares (109 acres) of peace and quiet, a cherished open space speckled with trees in this terribly dense city. Benches overlook small ponds, walking trails, and bike trails. See also the tour of Vondelpark on p 78. ⏱ *30 min. Enter through the gates on Stadhouderskade, at the corner of Vossiusstraat. Open 24 hr. Tram: 1, 2, 5, 7, or 10 to Leidseplein.*

⑥ ★★★ Anne Frankhuis. It's about a 30-minute walk from Vondelpark to the Anne Frank House (or you can catch a tram). It was in this typical Amsterdam canal house that a 13-year-old Anne Frank began to keep her famous diary. For 2 years during World War II, the Frank family and other Jewish refugees hid in near-total silence in these rooms, before they were betrayed and Nazi forces raided the house and deported them to concentration camps. You can see where young Anne pinned up photos of her favorite actress, Deanna Durbin, and view an original copy of Anne's diary. Protective Plexiglas panels have been placed over some walls, but little else has changed since the Franks lived here. Almost a million visitors a year tour this house; be prepared to spend some time waiting to enter. ⏱ *1½ hr. Arrive after 4pm to avoid long lines, especially in summer. Prinsengracht 263 (at Westermarkt).* ☎ *020/556-7105. www. annefrank.nl. Admission 7.50€ adults, 3.50€ kids 10–17. Mid-Mar to June and 1st 2 weeks in Sept Sun–Fri 9am–9pm, Sat 9am–10pm; July–Aug daily 9am–10pm; mid-Sept to mid-Mar daily 9am–7pm; Jan 1 & Dec 25 noon–7pm; May 4 9am–7pm; Dec 16 & 31 9am–5pm. Closed Yom Kippur. Tram: 13, 14, or 17 to Westermarkt.*

⑦ ★ De Prins. After a long day of sightseeing, relax with the locals at a traditional Dutch *eetcafé* (cafe with eats). One of my favorites is just across the canal from the Anne Frankhuis. Choose from a great selection of Dutch and Belgian beers, and select from an unpretentious but inventive Continental menu. *Prinsengracht 124.* ☎ *020/624-9382. $.*

The attic where Anne Frank and her family lived for 2 years.

The Best in **Two Days**

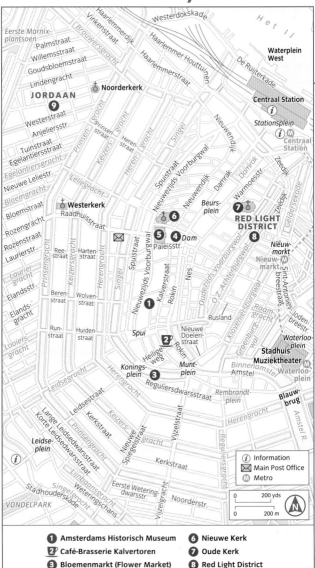

1 Amsterdams Historisch Museum
2 Café-Brasserie Kalvertoren
3 Bloemenmarkt (Flower Market)
4 Dam
5 Koninklijk Paleis (Royal Palace)
6 Nieuwe Kerk
7 Oude Kerk
8 Red Light District
9 Jordaan

Information
Main Post Office
M Metro

If you followed the "Best in One Day" tour, then you've already visited the most popular attractions and gotten an overview of the city from a canal cruise. Today you'll dig further into Amsterdam's history and architecture by visiting some of its monuments, smaller museums, and neighborhoods. You'll also stroll around the Flower Market and take a peek at the infamous Red Light District. START: Tram: 1, 2, 4, 5, 9, 14, 16, 24, or 25 to Spui.

① ★★ Amsterdams Historisch Museum (Amsterdam Historical Museum). Starting your day at this fascinating museum will give you a much deeper understanding of everything you'll see as you tour the city. The museum is housed in a former orphanage dating back to the 17th century (a small part of it dates back to 1578, when it was a convent). Gallery by gallery, century by century, you learn how a small fishing village founded around 1200 became a major sea power and trading center. Many exhibits focus on the 17th-century *Gouden Eeuw* (Golden Age), when Amsterdam was the richest city in the world. Art lovers will enjoy seeing famous paintings by Dutch masters explained in the context of their time and place in history. An intricate scale model from 1677 shows what is now the Royal Palace (stop ⑤ on this tour); some of its outer walls and the roof have been removed to give you a bird's-eye look inside. Lots of hands-on exhibits and some interesting video displays round out the experience. ⏱ 2 hr. Kalverstraat 92, Nieuwezijds Voorburgwal 357, and Sint-Luciënsteeg 27. ☎ 020/523-1822. www.ahm.nl. Admission 7€ adults, 5.25€ seniors, 3.50€ kids 6–18. Mon–Fri 10am–5pm; Sat–Sun and holidays 11am–5pm. Closed Jan 1, Apr 30, Dec 25. Tram: 1, 2, 4, 5, 9, 14, 16, 24, or 25 to Spui.

An exhibit hall in the Amsterdam Historical Museum.

and take in the heavenly 360-degree views of Amsterdam. If the weather is fine, you can grab a seat on the top-floor terrace, but the views from the floor-to-ceiling windows in the expansive lower dining room are equally panoramic. My favorite snack is a slathering of goat cheese on toasted focaccia with fresh tomatoes. The salade niçoise is excellent, and fried eggs with ham and cheese make a perfect late breakfast. *Top floor of the Kalvertoren mall, enter on Singel 457 and take the elevator to the 3rd floor.* ☎ 020/427-3901. Mon–Wed 10am–6:30pm, Thurs–Sat 10am–midnight, Sun 11am–6:30pm. $$.

② ★ Café-Brasserie Kalvertoren. I love to stop at the Kalvertoren in the late morning before the lunch rush

③ ★ Bloemenmarkt (Flower Market). Since you're in the heart of

Gardeners will enjoy choosing from the large variety of tulip bulbs at Amsterdam's Flower Market.

Amsterdam's main shopping street, Kalverstraat, you may want to spend some time browsing. When you've had your fill, head two streets south to the Singel canal (at Muntplein) where you'll find the Flower Market, which partially floats on a row of permanently moored barges, exploding with color and hundreds of flowers. Fresh tulips here cost about the same as those sold at the flower stands around town, so I don't recommend buying flowers and carrying them around all day. But it's a good place to pick up ready-to-travel packets of tulip bulbs that slip easily into your backpack or purse. *Singel (at Muntplein). Mon–Sat 9am–5:30pm, Sun*

11am–5:30pm. Tram: 4, 9, 14, 16, 24, or 25.

④ ★★ **Dam.** The Dam is the square that's the epicenter of Amsterdam. It's the site of the original dam built across the Amstel River in the 13th century, hence the name. It's not particularly grand—the surrounding buildings are a mix of architectural styles, and pedestrians, bikes, trams, and cars perpetually jam the surrounding streets. But several of the city's important monuments can be found here: the **Koninklijk Paleis, Nationaal Monument,** and the **Nieuwe Kerk.** Take a walk (beware of those trams!) around the Nationaal Monument, a white column erected in 1956 as a national tribute to Dutch citizens who died during the Nazi occupation during World War II. Urns filled with soil from the various provinces of the Netherlands and its former possessions overseas sit behind the monument (sculpted by Dutch artist John Radecker). 🕐 *15 min. Tram: 1, 2, 4, 5, 9, 13, 14, 16, 17, 24, or 25 to the Dam.*

⑤ ★ **Koninklijk Paleis (Royal Palace).** This is still the official residence of the reigning king or queen of the Netherlands, though Queen

The Dam.

The Oude Kerk (Old Church).

Beatrix and the other scions of the House of Orange prefer to live in The Hague. The palace (1648–55), originally designed as Amsterdam's Town Hall, has a solid, neoclassical facade. The building didn't become a palace until 1808. Its interior is filled with early-19th-century furniture, chandeliers, and marble floors. The most interesting room is the high-ceilinged Burgerzaal (Citizens' Chamber), where the maps inlaid on the marble floors show Amsterdam as the center of the world. The palace is closed to visitors during periods of royal residence and state receptions. **Note:** At this writing it was closed completely for renovations and due to reopen "from 2009." Until then it can be viewed only from the outside. 🕐 *1 hr. (when the palace reopens). Dam.* ☎ *020/620-4060. www.koninklijkhuis. nl. The following prices and hours were current when the palace was last open and may change. Admission 4.50€ adults; 3.60€ seniors, students & kids 6–16. Easter holidays & June–Aug daily 11am–5pm; Sept to mid-Dec & mid-Feb to May Tues–Thurs 12:30–5pm (days & hours vary with little or no notice; check before going).*

⑥ ★ Nieuwe Kerk (New Church). Originally built in the 14th century as the city's second Catholic Church, the Nieuwe Kerk was largely destroyed by fire in the 17th century (look for the carved gilded ceiling above the choir, which survived). A great deal of its original neo-Gothic grandeur has been restored, and all Dutch monarchs are inaugurated (not crowned!) here. Don't miss the elaborately carved altar and the great pipe organ (from about 1645), which is still used for concerts. In the south transept, the lower-right corner of the stained-glass windows depicts Queen Wilhelmina surrounded by courtiers at her inauguration. 🕐 *30 min. Dam (next to the Royal Palace).* ☎ *020/ 638-6909. www.nieuwekerk.nl. Admission varies with different events; free*

One of the Nieuwe Kerk's (New Church's) elaborate stained-glass windows.

The Royal Household

Although the queen's official residence is the Royal Palace, she does not own it, nor does she own any of her other residences. The state makes them available to her and allocates a budget of about 4,000,000€ per year to manage her royal household. Her salary is separate. She earns a net income of 750,000€; the amount is not taxable. She pays taxes only on her private assets—which, though difficult to calculate, are not substantial enough to make her one of richest women in the world, as was once thought.

when there's no special exhibit. Daily 10am–6pm.

⑦ ★★ Oude Kerk (Old Church).

A walk of several blocks east from the Nieuwe Kerk (into the Red Light District), brings you to the late-Gothic, triple-nave church, which was begun in 1250 and completed with the extension of the bell tower in 1566. Rembrandt's wife lies in vault 28K, which bears the simple inscription "Saskia Juni 1642." The magnificent 1728 open organ is regularly used for recitals. You can climb the church tower on a half-hourly guided tour (in English) for a great view of Old Amsterdam and the adjacent Red Light District. Just outside the Oude Kerk is what's claimed to be the world's first monument to prostitution. The

Old Church's famous organ.

bronze sculpture *Belle* (2007), depicts a hooker standing in a doorway and bears an inscription calling for "respect for sexworkers [sic] all over the world." ⏱ *30 min. Oudekerksplein (at Oudezijds Voorburgwal). ☎ 020/625-8284 church; 020/689-2565 tower. www.oudekerk.nl. Church: Admission 7€ adults, 5€ students, 1€ kids 5–18. Mon–Sat 11am–5pm; Sun 1–5pm. Tower: Admission 6€; minimum age 12. Apr–Sept Sat–Sun 1–5pm. Closed Jan 1 & Apr 30. Metro: Nieuwmarkt.*

⑧ Red Light District. Amster-

dam's *Rosse Buurt* (Red Light District) is one of its best-known "attractions," with red lights illuminating minimally clad prostitutes on display behind glass windows along medieval canals and alleyways. There are also live, hard-core sex shows that leave nothing to the imagination. Some visitors are repulsed by the sight of flesh for sale; for others it's just a fascinating window into the world's oldest profession. The Oude Kerk is in the middle of the Red Light District, so you can simply cross the canal and stroll up and down Oudezijds Achterburgwal. The very narrow alleyways leading away from the canal are also lined with glass "cages." It's not unsafe to meander here. You can skip it and head northwest from the Oude Kerk to Warmoesstraat, a pedestrian-only street lined with bars, funky sex shops (among them a "condomerie"),

A woman in the Red Light District waits for a customer.

and "coffee shops" where patrons are more likely to order marijuana than coffee. From Oudezijds Achterburgwal, head back toward the Oude Kerk, cross Oudezijds Voorburgwal and you'll hit Warmoesstraat. Continue north along the street and you'll find yourself facing Centraal Station.
⏱ *15–30 min. Dusk is the best time to visit, though it's open 24 hr. Metro: Nieuwmarkt.*

9 ★★ Jordaan. It feels miles away from the crowded, sometimes seedy center city where you've spent most of the day, yet the Jordaan is almost adjacent to Centraal Station and a great place to relax after a day of sightseeing. It's the most hip and unpretentiously elegant neighborhood in all of Amsterdam, its discreet canals lined with houseboats and its streets full of quaint boutiques and delightful cafes. If you have the time and energy, check out the walking tour of the Jordaan (p 52). Also consider staying for dinner (see chapter 6, "The Best Dining").

A Behind-the-Scenes Look at the Dutch Sex Industry

The Red Light District in Amsterdam dates back to the 13th century, when the city emerged as Europe's leading port and sailors returned from long trips desperate for female companionship. By 1850, with a little over 200,000 residents in the city, there were already over 200 brothels. Now, the sex industry is a $1-billion business in the Netherlands, (a minuscule piece of the $800 billion Dutch economy). To this day, there's debate within the government as to how to regulate this industry. In recent years, the city has been acting to rein in the sex industry and its links to organized crime, drugs, and human trafficking, by cutting the number of prostitutes' windows and sex clubs, and encouraging the spread of "normal" life in the Red Light District. Some of the more mundane rules change constantly (such as: Can a prostitute claim lingerie on her income tax as a business write-off?), but the health department is very strict with its regulations. There are rules on everything from how hot the water needs to be before a prostitute washes her underwear to how long the women's nails can be. The women come from all walks of life and for some this is just a second job to earn extra cash. Some are young students, some are housewives. Women that you see in windows in the Red Light District can expect to earn 60€ to 150€ per customer, depending on what is asked of them. High-class prostitutes (found through an upmarket escort service or luxury brothel) can pull in over 1,000€ a night.

The Best in **Three Days**

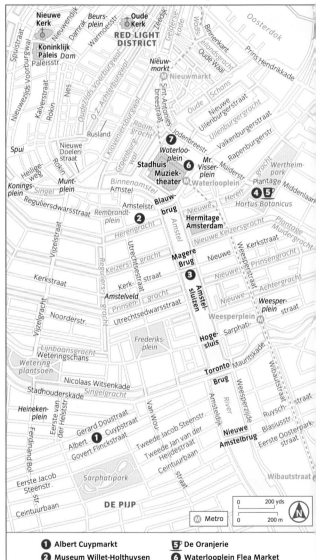

1 Albert Cuypmarkt
2 Museum Willet-Holthuysen
3 Magere Brug (Skinny Bridge)
4 Hortus Botanicus
5 De Oranjerie
6 Waterlooplein Flea Market
7 Museum Het Rembrandthuis

If you've followed the "Best in One" and "Best in Two Days" tours, then you've already seen many of the city's highlights. It's time to slow down a bit, blend in with the locals, meander around the markets, and take in some smaller museums. On this tour you'll also get a chance to (literally) stop and smell the roses at the relaxing Botanical Garden. START: **Tram 16, 24, or 25 to Albert Cuypstraat.**

The carefully restored kitchen at the Museum Willet-Holthuysen.

1 ★ **Albert Cuypmarkt.** I love coming to the Albert Cuyp Market in the morning, getting lost in the frenzy of shoppers, and marveling at the rows of fresh fish, fruit, vegetables, and textiles on display. The street market lies along Albert Cuypstraat in the heart of De Pijp, a residential neighborhood that has a mixed population of young professionals and ethnic minorities, many of the latter hailing (though it may be several generations back) from the former Dutch colony of Suriname. The area is slightly more affordable than the Jordaan and therefore attracts a somewhat younger crowd. Along the streets that intersect Albert Cuypstraat, you'll find many cafes where you can get a quick pick-me-up of strong coffee or tea. ⏲ *1 hr. Albert Cuypstraat, between Van Woustraat & Ferdinand Bolstraat. Mon–Sat 9am–6pm. Tram: 16 or 24 to Albert Cuypstraat.*

2 ★ **Museum Willet-Holthuysen.** This is one of the best-preserved 17th-century canal houses in Amsterdam. It was built in 1687 and

Fun Facts & Figures

In Amsterdam you'll find one million permanent residents; more than a million visitors each month; 600,000 flower bulbs in its parks and public gardens; 1,281 bridges (8 of them wooden drawbridges); 600,000 bicycles; 220,000 trees; 260 city trams; 6,800 16th-, 17th-, and 18th-century buildings; 1,400 cafes and bars; 755 restaurants; 206 paintings by van Gogh; and 22 paintings by Rembrandt.

Skinny Bridge at night.

renovated several times before its last owner, Louisa Willet-Holthuysen, willed the mansion and her fine-art collection to the city in 1885. Among the most interesting rooms are a Victorian-era bedroom on the second floor, a large reception room with tapestry wall panels, and an 18th-century basement kitchen set up to look as though the cook has just stepped out to go shopping. Be sure to peek out at the impressively restored 18th-century formal garden. ⏱ *45 min. Herengracht 605 (near the Amstel River).* ☎ *020/523-1822. www. willetholthuysen.nl. Admission 5€ adults, 3.75€ seniors, 2.50€ kids 6–18. Mon–Fri 10am–5pm; Sat–Sun*

11am–5pm. Closed Jan 1, Apr 30 & Dec 25. Tram: 4, 9, or 14 to Rembrandtplein.

❸ ★ **Magere Brug (Skinny Bridge).** After leaving the museum, head west toward the Amstel, and then south along the riverbank for a quick 15-minute detour to see this fantastic bridge. Legend has it that the Magere Brug was built to make it easier for two sisters (of the Mager family) who lived on opposite sides of the river to visit each other—but *mager* also means "thin" in Dutch, hence the nickname. The double drawbridge was built in 1670 of African azobe wood; it was last renovated in 1969. Come during the day to see the unusual wood details, or at night to see it twinkling with hundreds of lights. If you're lucky, you might see the bridge master raising it to allow boats through. ⏱ *15 min. The bridge spans the Amstel btw. Kerkstraat & Nieuwe Kerkstraat.*

❹ ★ **kids Hortus Botanicus (Botanical Garden).** On the right (east) bank of the river, go northeast to this oasis of green, a treasure trove of tropical plants taken from (among other places) the former Dutch colonies of Indonesia, Suriname, and the Antilles. Established in 1682, this lovely garden explodes with the

The butterfly house at the Botanical Garden is a big hit with kids.

Waterlooplein Flea Market.

colors and scents of over 250,000 flowers and 115,000 plants and trees. The city's physicians and apothecaries originally created it as a garden for medicinal herbs. The first coffee plant in Europe was brought here in 1706 by a Dutch merchant who smuggled it out of Ethiopia. The three-climate greenhouse gets progressively warmer as you walk through it—most of the plants here come from Australia and South Africa. There's also an herb garden, a desert greenhouse, and a butterfly house with free-flying giant butterflies that kids will love. ⏱ *1 hr. Plantage Middenlaan 2A.* ☎ *020/625-9021. www.dehortus.nl. Admission 7€ adults, 3.50€ seniors & kids 5–14. Feb–June & Sept–Nov Mon–Fri 9am–5pm, Sat–Sun 10am–5pm; July–Aug Mon–Fri 9am–7pm, Sat–Sun 10am–7pm; Dec–Jan Mon–Fri 9am–4pm, Sat–Sun 10am–4pm. Closed Jan 1 & Dec 25. Tram: 9 or 14 to Plantage Middenlaan.*

5 ★ **De Oranjerie.** This cafe, in Hortus Botanicus, is one of my absolute favorite places to unwind and recharge. It's housed in the beautiful 1875 Oranjerie building, designed to shelter citrus trees in winter. The cafe serves one of the best apple pies in the city, along with delicious salads and imaginative sandwiches. If you score one of the outdoor tables, you can listen to the birds chirping as you eat. *Inside Hortus Botanicus, Plantage Middenlaan 2A.* ☎ *020/ 625-9021. Daily 11am–4pm. $$.*

6 ★ **Waterlooplein Flea Market.** Another 10-minute walk brings you to this quintessentially classic Amsterdam flea market. In its glory, before World War II, you could find amazing antiques and maybe even paintings by the masters at bargain prices. Today you can meander from one merchant's tent to another, hunting for good deals on anything from cooking pots to used CDs, leather jackets, watches, and colorful sweaters. I come here just to people-watch. It's also a good place to try some street food, like french fries eaten Dutch style—with mayonnaise. ⏱ *30 min. Waterlooplein. Mon–Sat 10am–5pm. Tram: 9 or 14 to Waterloo-plein.*

7 ★★ **Museum Het Rembrandthuis (Rembrandt House Museum).** Just around the corner from Waterlooplein lies the beautifully preserved house where the artist Rembrandt van Rijn lived and worked in the 17th century. He bought the three-story house in 1639 when he was Amsterdam's most fashionable portrait painter. In this house, Rembrandt's son Titus was born and his wife Saskia died (you may have seen her tomb at the Oude Kerk yesterday). Due to his extravagant lifestyle, Rembrandt was bankrupt when he left the house in 1658, and it wasn't until 1906 that the building was restored as a museum. Today the old house looks the way it did when Rembrandt lived and worked here—the 17th-century furnishings closely match the detailed descriptions Rembrandt gave of his possessions in his 1656 bankruptcy petition. You'll see the kitchen and maid's bedroom on the ground floor, and upstairs you'll find Rembrandt's bedroom, living room, and the studio, where he painted such works as his famous *Nightwatch*. You can also see his printing press and some 250 of his etchings and drawings, which hang on the walls. 🕐 *1 hr. Arrive here 1–2 hr. before closing to avoid the crowds. Visit on Wed or weekends to see etching demonstrations.*

Rembrandt House Museum.

Jodenbreestraat 4–6 (at Waterlooplein). ☎ 020/520-0400. www.rembrandthuis.nl. Admission 8€ adults, 5.50€ students, 1.50€ kids 6–15. Daily 10am–5pm. Closed Jan. 1. Tram: 9 or 14 to Waterlooplein. ●

Below Sea Level

Amsterdammers have always had an intimate relationship with the sea. All those centuries of listening to the waves beating against the dikes raised against its clear and present danger—how could it be otherwise? But that its solid, timeless buildings stand, and its 750,000 inhabitants live, where waves should by all rights be lapping, is a difficult concept for foreigners to grasp.

Amsterdam lies up to 5.5m (18 ft.) below mean sea level. That it does not lie beneath the sea is due to stringent protective measures and Dutch engineering skill, which together have kept the city's collective head above water for most of the past 800 years.

If the coast defenses that protect Amsterdam should ever be overwhelmed, most of the city would vanish beneath the waves (did you check that insurance policy?). A graphic cross-section of the topography between the North Sea and Amsterdam, which you can buy printed on postcards and posters, shows that Vondelpark would become a lake, the Metro tunnels would be well and truly drowned, and the trams would float away, but if you happened to be standing on top of the Oude Kerk tower you wouldn't even get your feet wet.

Amsterdam for Art Lovers

ⓘ Information
Ⓜ Metro

| 0 | 200 yds |
| 0 | 200 m |

Waterplein West

Het IJ

Centraal Station ⓘ

Stationsplein ⓘ Ⓜ Centraal Station

JAVA-EILAND

Muziekgebouw aan 't IJ/ Bimhuis

Passenger Terminal Amsterdam

IJhaven

De Ruijterkade

Piet Heinkade

6

IJ-Tunnel

Oosterdokskade **5**

Dijksgracht

Oude Kerk

RED LIGHT DISTRICT

Oosterdok

NEMO

MARINE ETABLISSEMENT (NAVAL COMPLEX)

Kattenburgerstraat

Nieuw-markt

Prins Hendrikkade

Maritime Museum

Kattenburger-vaart

Nieuwmarkt

Sint-Antonies-breestraat

Oude Schans

Binnenkant

Kloveniersburgwal

Raamgracht

Nieuwe Uilenburgerstraat

Uilenburgergracht

Valkenburgerstraat

Rapenburgerstr.

Hoogtekadijk

Nieuwe Vaart

Jodenbree-straat

Plantage Doklaan

Waterloo-plein

Stadhuis

Muziek-theater Ⓜ Waterlooplein

Mr. Visser-plein Muiderstr.

Wertheim-park

Entrepotdok

Plantage Kerklaan

Binnen-amstel Amstel

Blauw-brug

Nieuwe Herengracht

Hortus Botanicus

ARTIS ZOO

Heren-gracht

Keizers-gracht **3**

Utrechtsestr.

Nieuwe Keizersgracht

Plantage Muidergracht

Plantage Middenlaan

2

Kerkstraat

Plantage Muidergracht

Amstel

Nieuwe

Kerk-straat **4**

Magere Brug

Weesperstraat

Prinsengracht

Prinsengracht

Nieuwe

Nieuwe Achtergracht

Sarphatistraat

Singelgracht

Utrechtsedwarsstr.

Amstel-sluizen River

Weesperplein Ⓜ

Weesper-plein

Mauritskade

Frederiks-plein

Hoge-sluis

Sajet-plein

Boerhaave-plein

OOSTERPARK

Toronto Brug

's-Gravesande-plein

Wibautstraat

Ruyschstraat

1

1 Cobra Museum

2 Hermitage Amsterdam

3 Sluizer

4 Kerkstraat

5 Stedelijk Museum CS

6 Fifteen

Previous page: An Englishman in Moscow, *by Kazimir Severinovich Malevich.*

Amsterdam is a feast for art lovers. With 22 Rembrandts, 206 van Goghs, numerous Vermeers, and a plethora of Impressionist and post-Impressionist paintings scattered throughout the city, art lovers will be in heaven here. This tour is for art lovers who would have already made a beeline to the top museums and are ready to dig deeper into all the art riches that Amsterdam has to offer. Today you'll have a chance to get off the beaten path to see works unique to this area; contemporary works by local, living artists; and the Schuttersgalerij with its outsized canvases depicting well-to-do members of 17th-century Civic Guards companies. START: **Cobra Museum (in Amstelveen); tram no. 5 to Binnenhof or Metro line 51 to the Amstelveen Centrum stop.**

1 ★ **Cobra Museum.** Art lovers will find this breathtakingly modern museum worth the trek to its off-the-beaten-path location (I recommend taking a 15-min. taxi ride or 20-min. tram ride from the center city straight here and back—leafy, suburban Amstelveen is not the most scenic area of Amsterdam). The museum (1995), designed by Dutch architect Wim Quist, overflows with the post–World War II abstract expressionist art of the Cobra group, named for the initials of the founding artists' home cities: Copenhagen, Brussels, and Amsterdam. Karel Appel (1921–2006) was the Dutchman, a controversial painter, sculptor, and graphic artist. As is true of many Cobra artists, Appel's work, including *Child and Beast II* (1951), has a childlike quality, employing bright colors and abstract shapes. He once said, "I paint like a barbarian in a barbarous age." The building's abundant natural light and open space creates a perfect home for the modern art found here. ⏱ *2 hr. Sandbergplein 1, Amstelveen.* ☎ *020/547-5050. www.cobra-museum.nl. Admission 9.50€ adults, 6.50€ seniors, 5€ kids 6–18. Tues–Sun 11am–5pm. Closed Jan 1, Apr 30 & Dec 25. Tram: 5 to Binnenhof. Metro: line 51 to Amstelveen Centrum.*

The Cobra Museum's starkly modern interior complements the art displayed here.

The Hermitage.

❷ ★ Hermitage Amsterdam.

Take a taxi or tram back to the center of town to the Amsterdam branch of Russia's State Hermitage museum of art and fine arts, which opened in 2004. It affords you a glimpse into the rich collection previously found only in St. Petersburg. Housed in the neo-classical 1681 Amstelhof (which is flanked on two sides by canals and on a third by the Amstel River), the exhibits here change every 6 months. The Hermitage owns over three million items (of which over 600 are paintings by Dutch and Flemish masters), so you have an excellent chance of seeing some masterpieces on loan from St. Petersburg. ⏱ *1½ hr. Nieuwe Herengracht 14 (at the Amstel River).* ☎ *020/530-8755. www.hermitage.nl. Admission 7€ adults, free for kids under 17. Daily 10am–5pm. Closed Jan 1, Apr 30 & Dec 25. Tram: 9 or 14 to Waterlooplein.*

❸ Sluizer.

A few minutes' walk from the Amstel River, you'll find this casual eatery with two dining rooms. One is an old-fashioned brasserie serving simple French fare. The other serves seafood in an Art Deco dining room, with daily specials ranging from plain cod or eel to scallops and crab casseroles. *Utrechtsestraat 41–45 (btw. Herengracht & Keizersgracht).* ☎ *020/622-6376. $$.*

❹ Visiting local art galleries.

After leaving the Hermitage, stretch your legs and take in some fresh air as you stroll down the banks of the Amstel River to Kerkstraat (about a 10-min. walk). Turn right on Kerkstraat and you'll find a charming narrow street lined with galleries devoted to contemporary Dutch art. Foremost among them is ArtaCasa (☎ 020/639-3213), which changes its exhibits every season. ⏱ *1½ hr. Gallery hours vary, but most are open 1–6pm Tues–Sat.*

❺ Schuttersgalerij (Civic Guards Gallery).

If you don't feel like visiting the Amsterdam Historical Museum (p. 11) but are craving some historic art and architecture, stroll through the Schuttersgalerij (Civic Guards Gallery), a narrow, two-story sky-lit, passageway linking Kalverstraat to the hidden Begijnhof courtyard (p. 24). It's not easy to find but it is signed at various points around the museum. Under the walkway's glass roof, you'll see 15 bigger-is-better, 17th-century paintings showing the city's heroic musketeers, the Civic Guards. Elegantly uniformed and of doubtful military effectiveness, these militia companies had once played an important role in the city's defense, but by this time had degenerated into little more than puffed-up banqueting societies. The paintings are in the same tradition, if not quite the same league, as Rembrandt's *The Night Watch,* but then you don't have to line up and pay to view them. And seen in this relaxed context, without crowds, they are well worth the detour. One of the best is Govert Flinck's *The Company of Captain Joan Huydecoper Celebrating the Peace of Münster* (1648). ⏱ *20 min. Outside the Amsterdams Historisch Museum, between Sint-Luciënsteeg and Gedempte Begijnensloot. No* *phone. Free admission. Mon–Fri 10am–5pm, Sat–Sun 11am–5pm. Closed Jan 1. Tram: 1, 2, 4, 5, 9, 16, 24, or 25 to Spui.*

6 ★★ **Fifteen.** For an unrivaled ending to your day, take tram no. 26 from nearby Centraal Station three stops east to celeb British chef Jamie Oliver's popular restaurant/ trattoria Fifteen. Though Oliver rarely presides in person, his signature breezy yet professional approach permeates both the service and the fusiony Mediterranean cuisine, in a setting that artfully combines graffiti, sheet metal, and white table linens. *Pakhuis Amsterdam, Jollemanhof 9.* ☎ *0900/343-8336. Restaurant daily 6–11pm (closed Sun mid-July to mid Aug); trattoria Sun–Thurs 5:30–11pm. $$–$$$.*

The Civic Guards Gallery.

The Best Special-Interest Tours

Architectural Amsterdam

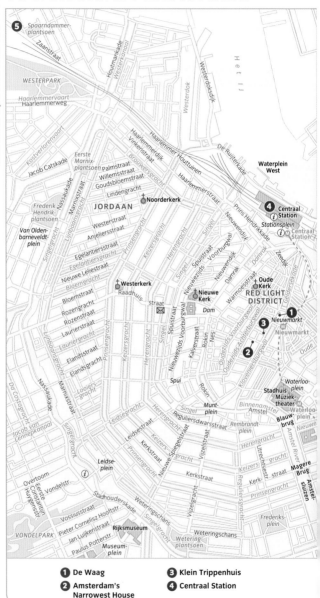

1 De Waag
2 Amsterdam's Narrowest House
3 Klein Trippenhuis
4 Centraal Station

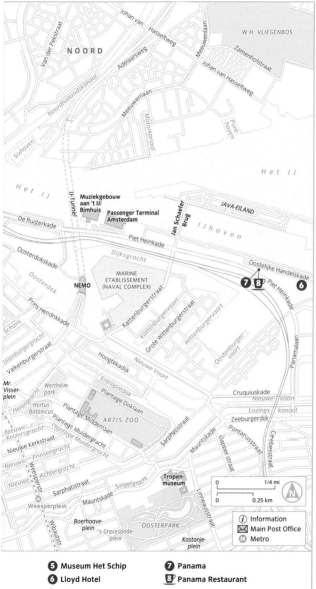

5 Museum Het Schip

6 Lloyd Hotel

7 Panama

8 Panama Restaurant

There are so many architectural styles in Amsterdam that the city can seem quite schizophrenic at times. Architecture buffs can entertain themselves just by walking the streets or taking a tram ride in any corner of the city. On this tour you'll get an overview of the major schools of architecture, starting with medieval, but I've focused on examples from the Amsterdam School, the unique movement that forever changed the look of the city in the early decades of the 20th century. START: **Metro to Nieuwmarkt.**

❶ De Waag. On the fringe of what is now the city's Chinatown, you'll find Amsterdam's only surviving medieval fortified gate. Built in the 14th century, it later became a public weigh house and then a guild house. One of the guilds lodged here was the Surgeon's Guild, immortalized in Rembrandt's painting *The Anatomy Lesson* (1632), which depicts a dissection being conducted in the upper-floor Theatrum Anatomicum. This part of De Waag is rarely open, but you can meander inside the historic ground-floor restaurant (good international fare), called In de Waag. ⏱ *15 min. Nieuwmarkt. Metro: Nieuwmarkt.*

Amsterdam's narrowest house.

❷ Amsterdam's Narrowest House. Walk toward the Dam to take a look at one of the city's narrowest houses at Oude Hoogstraat 22. The house has a typical Amsterdam bell gable and is only 2m (6½ ft.) wide and 6m (20 ft.) deep. ⏱ *10 min. Oude Hoogstraat 22.*

❸ Klein Trippenhuis. Nearby you'll find the cornice-gabled Klein Trippenhuis, dubbed "Mr. Trip's Coachman's House." This house is only 2.4m (7¾ ft.) wide. It faces the elegant Trippenhuis at no. 29, which at 22m (72 ft.) is the widest Old Amsterdam house, and was built in 1660 for the wealthy Trip brothers. The story goes that their coachman exclaimed one day: "Oh, if only I could be so lucky as to have a house as wide as my master's door." His master overheard this, and the coachman's wish was granted. The house is now a fashion boutique. ⏱ *10 min. Kloveniersburgwal 26.*

❹ Centraal Station. Take a 15-minute walk or jump on any of the trams heading north to Centraal Station, an architectural masterpiece. Designed by architect Petrus Josephus Hubertus Cuypers, it was built between 1884 and 1889 on three artificial islands, which themselves are supported on 30,000 pilings. At the time of its construction, Amsterdammers thoroughly disliked the station, but now the major transportation hub is an attraction in its own right, partly for its extravagant Dutch neo-Renaissance facade and

Centraal Station, Amsterdam's transportation hub.

partly for the liveliness that permanently surrounds it. ⏲ *10 min. Tram: 1, 2, 4, 5, 9, 13, 16, 17, 24, 25, or 26 to Centraal Station.*

5 Museum Het Schip. From Centraal Station, take bus no. 22 heading west (about a 20-min. ride)

to the city's most famous example of an Amsterdam School building. The movement's designs, which were influenced by socialist ideas and a reaction to the bourgeois and neo-Gothic architecture of the time, can be recognized by a heavy

Amsterdam's Canal Houses

As you walk around the city's canals, you'll begin to notice that not all canal houses are the same—though they all may look similar. If you look closely, you'll notice a wonderful mix of architectural detail ranging from classical to Renaissance to modern. Most of Amsterdam's 6,800 landmark buildings have gables. These hide the pitched roofs and demonstrate the architect's vertical showmanship in a city where hefty property taxes and expensive canalfront land encouraged pencil-thin buildings.

Around 600 old *gevelstenen* (gable stones)—ornamental tiles, sculptures, or reliefs that often play on the original owner's name or profession—remain. Walls in the Begijnhof and on Sint-Luciënsteeg at the **Amsterdams Historisch Museum** (see p 11, ❶) have some good gable stones, including the oldest known (from 1603), showing a milkmaid balancing her buckets.

Incidentally, the *hijsbalk*—the hook you see on many gables—might look to be ideal for a hanging, but it is actually used with rope and pulley for hauling large, heavy items into and out of homes that have steep, narrow staircases.

A window at Museum Het Schip, one of the best examples of the Amsterdam School of architecture.

reliance on brickwork, elaborate masonry, painted glass, and wrought-iron work. Of the dozen or so architects who were part of this school, Michel de Klerk (1884–1923) was the most influential. The museum dedicates itself entirely to the architecture of the Amsterdam School and is housed in a former post office built in 1919 and designed by de Klerk. The post office was only a small part of this large boatlike building (hence its nickname, "the Ship"): It also contained 102 small homes for the working class. The museum features a very interesting exhibit about the Amsterdam School's sources of inspiration and explains the social conditions in the Netherlands during World War I that allowed this school of architecture to flourish. A newly restored wing originally housed working-class members of a socialist association in the 1920s and provides an intimate view of the Amsterdam School's unique designs. The renovation boasts original woodwork and colors, plus furniture and utensils identical to the ones used in the '20s—even the closets have been restored to their original style. ⏱ *30 min. Spaarndammerplantsoen 140.* ☎ *020/418-2885. www.het schip.nl. Admission 5€ adults, 2.75€ seniors, 2€ students. Wed–Sun 1–5pm. Bus: 22 West to Zaanstraat (last stop).*

6 Lloyd Hotel. Hop on the bus back to Centraal Station and connect to tram no. 26 for a quick ride to the East Docklands area, an

The Lloyd Hotel.

up-and-coming neighborhood (it's about a 30-min. walk east from Centraal Station). Here, old run-down warehouses and large, abandoned historic buildings are being transformed at a maddening pace as the area fills with young professionals scared away by the cramped spaces and high rents in Central Amsterdam. Leave the tram at Rietlandpark and walk across the park to the renovated building housing the Lloyd Hotel. This Amsterdam School building was constructed in 1917 and served as a "waiting room" after World War I for migrant families heading from Eastern Europe to South America. The ground-floor lobby was a high-ceilinged dining room that would seat 350 immigrants. You can walk around these rooms now and take in the stunning renovation, completed in 2004, that transformed this historical space into Amsterdam's most avant-garde hotel (see p 129 for a review of the hotel). During World War II, the Germans used this building as a prison, and from 1964 to 1989 it was a detention center for juvenile delinquents. 🕐 *30 min. Oostelijke Handelskade 34.* ☎ *020/561-3636. www.lloydhotel.com. Tram: 10 or 26 to Rietlandpark.*

❼ ★ Panama. Leaving the Lloyd, make a left and walk a few minutes down to the end of the street. Here, you'll find Club Panama, housed in a former power station built around 1899. Today it's one of the city's trendiest venues, with a happening bar, divine restaurant, and celebrated nightclub (see p 108 for a full review). *Oostelijke Handelskade 4.* ☎ *020/311-8686. www.panama.nl. Tram: 10 or 26 to Rietlandpark.*

❽ Panama Restaurant. Wrap up your tour with a drink in the Panama's fantastic loungelike bar while gazing out floor-to-ceiling windows that overlook the river. The bar has a good selection of appetizers and light meals. You can lounge an afternoon or evening away here, watching the preppy after-work crowd sipping on martinis. *Oostelijke Handelskade 4.* ☎ *020/311-8686. $$.*

Urban Minefield

In such a beautiful city, with high gables in many and varied shapes and forms, there's a temptation to walk along gazing upward. Be careful. There's the possibility you'll walk straight into a canal, but that's a minor danger compared to the one underfoot. Many Amsterdammers have dogs, some of them the size of Shetland ponies. Signs on the sidewalk saying HOND IN DE GOOT (DOG IN THE GUTTER) are mostly ignored by both owner and dog. Take your eye off the ground for so much as an instant and you (and your footwear) might regret it.

Amsterdam with Kids

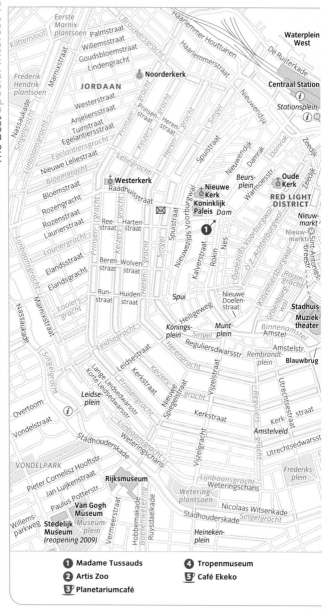

1 Madame Tussauds
2 Artis Zoo
3 Planetariumcafé

4 Tropenmuseum
5 Café Ekeko

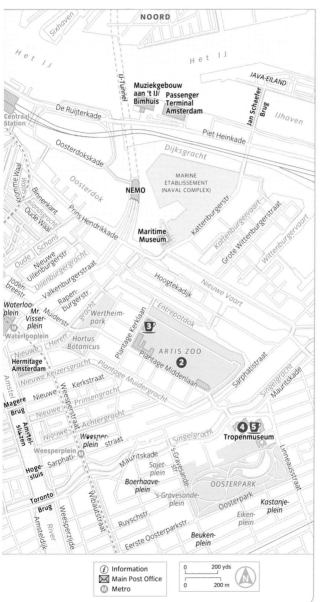

0   200 yds
0   200 m

Kids will have plenty to gawk at while walking around Amsterdam—the many houseboats lining the canals and the big barges chugging along the river fascinate children, and a ride on a tram can be an attraction in itself. You may also want to take them on the Maritime City tour (later in this chapter), especially if they're over 5. START: **Tram, 4, 9, 14, 16, 24, or 25 to the Dam.**

❶ ★ Madame Tussauds. Spend a frivolous morning at this popular museum. You'll see all the waxen celebrities you'd expect, plus the many hands-on activities that make this museum a winner for kids. In the Be the Next Idol exhibit, modeled after the popular TV show, you sing a tune of your choice and hear what the jury says about you. In the Royalty section, kids can wear tiaras and crowns and have their pictures taken with a wax Queen Beatrix. As you walk around, you'll see celebs from all eras and walks of life, from Charlie Chaplin, Picasso, van Gogh, and Marilyn Monroe to George W. Bush, Nelson Mandela, Madonna, and Harrison Ford as Indiana Jones. ⏱ *2 hr. Arrive right at opening time to avoid the crowds. Dam 20.* ☎ *020/ 522-1010. www.madametussauds.nl. Admission 20€ adults, 15€ kids 5–15. Open hours vary (see calendar on website); generally mid-July to*

mid-Aug daily 10am–11pm; mid-Aug to mid-July daily 10am–6:30pm. Closed Apr 30. Tram: 4, 9, 14, 16, 24, or 25 to the Dam.

❷ ★★ Artis Zoo. Amsterdam's fantastic zoo, established in 1838, is huge—over 14 hectares (35 acres)—so I suggest buying a map at the entrance and targeting the animals your kids want to see most. With two restaurants and several cafes to choose from, you can easily spend the whole day here. There are over 6,000 animals and 1,400 species. You can spot giraffes at the African Savannah and llamas and guanacos in the South American Pampas. Most kids love the chimpanzees; the zoo rotates the animals on display so they—the animals, that is—never seem tired or bored with the visiting throngs. Try to catch one of these daily feedings: The European vultures are fed

Seals at the Artis Zoo.

at 11am, sea lions at 11:30am and 3:45pm, pelicans at 2:30pm, and penguins at 3:30pm. Crocodiles are fed on Sunday only at 2:30pm. Included in the admission is entry to Artis's Aquarium (1882), Planetarium, Insect House, and Geological Museum. There's also a children's farm, where kids can pet assorted Dutch animals. 🕐 *3–5 hr. Plantage Kerklaan 38–40 (at Plantage Middenlaan).* ☎ *020/523-3400. www.artis. nl. Admission 18€ adults, 17€ seniors, 15€ kids 3–9. July–Aug Sun–Fri 9am–6pm, Sat 9am–10pm; Sept–June daily 9am–5pm. Tram: 9 or 14 to Plantage Kerklaan.*

3️⃣ **Planetariumcafé.** If it's a nice day and you're headed to the zoo, fuel up for your visit by taking a break at this fun eatery inside the

These photos of Anne Frank were taken around 1940.

"A Voice Within Me Is Sobbing"

The handsome merchant house where the Frank family lived faces one of the city's most charming canals. The house was built in 1653 and doubled as a warehouse. Otto Frank, who moved his family here from Frankfurt, Germany, in 1933, stored his herbs and spices in the front of the house. The back of the house (in Dutch, the *Achterhuis*), known as the Secret Annex, later became the family's hiding place. For 25 months, the Frank family (father Otto, his wife Edith, and their two daughters Margot and Anne) and four family friends hid from Nazi invaders. The hideaway was concealed from the front of the house by a moveable bookcase. Anne began writing in her diary on her birthday, June 12, 1942. Her last entry was on August 1, 1944, shortly before Nazi police raided the hideaway and the family was sent to separate concentration camps. Anne and Margot died of typhus at Bergen-Belsen. Only Otto survived the camps. He returned to the house after the war and fulfilled Anne's wishes to have her diary published. The first edition, in Dutch, appeared in 1947. Since then, Anne's diary has been published in over 60 languages.

Older kids, especially those who have read *The Diary of Anne Frank*, will be interested in seeing the house where Anne and her family hid for 2 harrowing years. For information on visiting the Anne Frankhuis, see p 9, 6️⃣.

Kids may not appreciate NEMO's unique architecture, but they're sure to enjoy the hands-on exhibits inside.

planetarium. Fill up on tasty sandwiches and other snacks while looking at the stars and planets. There's also a video arcade. *Inside Artis Zoo Planetarium.* ☎ 020/523-3400. $.

④ ★★ Tropenmuseum (Tropical Museum). Holland's Royal Institute for the Tropics owns this unusual museum devoted to the study of the cultures of tropical areas around the world. Its focus reflects Holland's former role as a landlord in such

The Tropenmuseum has a special department just for kids.

countries as Indonesia, Suriname, and the Caribbean islands of (among others) Curaçao, St. Maarten, Bonaire, and Aruba. The building itself is noteworthy for its heavily ornamented 19th-century facade featuring turrets, stepped gables, arched windows, and delicate spires, and a monumental galleried interior court. Of the exhibits, the most fascinating for kids are the walk-through model villages and city-street scenes that capture a moment in daily life. You can stroll through a Nigerian village, an Arab souk, and a traditional yurt tent home of nomads in central Asia. You'll also see fantastic wedding costumes from Thailand and Turkey and bridal jewelry from Northern Sumatra. In Tropenmuseum Junior, kids learn about tropical countries and their people through stories, dances, games, and paintings. This part of the museum is only open to kids ages 6 to 12 (and one adult per child). Tropenmuseum Junior is open Wednesday, Saturday, Sunday, national holidays, and during all school holidays. ⏱ *2 hr. Linnaeusstraat 2 (at Mauritskade).* ☎ *020/658-8200. www.tropen museum.nl. Admission 7.50€ adults; 6€ seniors & students; 4€ kids 6–17. Daily 10am–5pm (to 3pm Dec 5, 24 & 31). Closed Jan 1, Apr 30, May 5 &*

Dec 25. Tram: 7, 9, 10, or 14 to Mauritskade.

5 Café Ekeko. Adjacent to Tropenmuseum Junior, this lively cafe is a perfect place to sample a drink and a meal or snack from one of the tropical countries you're about to visit. The changing menu might include such specialties as vegetable samosas from India, a Thai beef salad, or Caribbean chicken with rice. *Inside the Tropenmuseum. $.*

A Rainy-Day Option

If you find yourself with a rainy afternoon and stir-crazy kids on your hands, head to **NEMO** (Oosterdok 2, off Prins Hendrikkade, over the south entrance to the IJ Tunnel; ☎ 0900/919-1100; www.e-nemo.nl). This swooping, modern building, designed by Italian architect Renzo Piano, looks like a graceful oceangoing ship. NEMO is as much a hands-on experience as it is a museum, as evidenced by its motto: Forbidden Not to Touch. It's a great experience for kids 9 or older. Through games, experiments, and demonstrations, kids learn how to steer a supertanker safely into port, execute a complicated surgical procedure, blow a soap bubble large enough to stand inside, and more. Exhibits answer questions like: Why is water clear but the ocean blue? Why does toothpaste contain sugar? In Bits & Co, NEMO's digital world, you can don a virtual-reality helmet and play with images, sounds, and websites. The broad, sloping stairway to NEMO's roof is an attraction in itself, a place to hang out and take in the magnificent views. At the top, you are 30m (98 ft.) above the IJ channel and have sweeping views over the Old Harbor and Eastern Dock. Moored alongside is an immense replica of the United East India Company (V.O.C.) merchant ship *Amsterdam*, which foundered off Hastings, England, in 1749 on her maiden voyage to Indonesia, and moved here from its usual berth across the water at the temporarily closed Maritime Museum (see "Maritime Amsterdam," below). You can climb aboard and explore every nook and cranny. Reenactors create scenes from everyday life on the ship. Sailors fire cannons, sing sea shanties, mop the deck, hoist cargo on board, and attend a solemn "burial at sea." You can watch sailmakers and rope makers at work and see the cook prepare a shipboard meal in the galley. Admission to NEMO is 12€ for adults; free for kids under 4. It's open daily from 10am to 5pm July and August, and during other school vacations; Tuesday to Sunday from 10am to 5pm September through June. The museum is closed January 1, April 30, and December 25. Admission to the V.O.C. ship *Amsterdam* is 5€ for ages 4 and up, or 2€ if you already have a ticket for NEMO.

Maritime Amsterdam

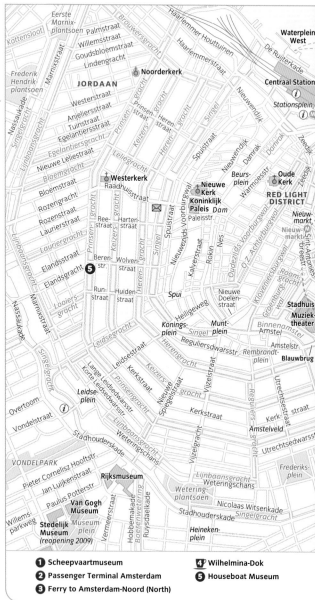

1 Scheepvaartmuseum
2 Passenger Terminal Amsterdam
3 Ferry to Amsterdam-Noord (North)
4 Wilhelmina-Dok
5 Houseboat Museum

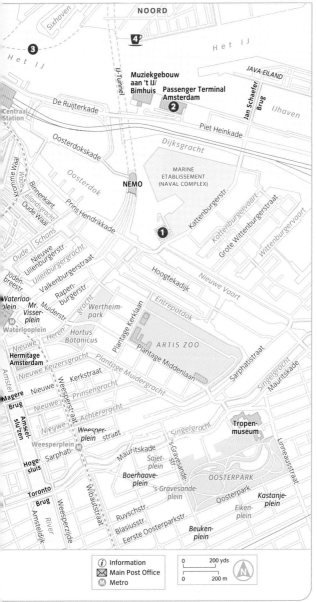

NOORD

Het IJ

Het IJ

3

4

JAVA-EILAND

IJ-Tunnel

Muziekgebouw aan 't IJ/ Bimhuis

Passenger Terminal Amsterdam
2

Jan Schaefer Brug

IJhaven

De Ruijterkade

Piet Heinkade

Centraal Station

Oosterdokskade

Dijksgracht

Komme Waal

Wallis

Oosterdok

NEMO

MARINE ETABLISSEMENT (NAVAL COMPLEX)

Binnenkant

Eilandsgracht

Oude Waal

Prins Hendrikkade

Kattenburgerstr.

1

Kattenburgervaart

Grote Wittenburgerstraat

Wittenburgervaart

Oude Schans

Nieuwe Uilenburgerstr.

Uilenburgergracht

Valkenburgerstraat

Hoogtekadijk

Nieuwe Vaart

Joden-breestr.

Rapen-burgerstr.

gracht

Werthein-park

Waterloo-plein

Mr. Visser-plein

M Waterlooplein

Heren

Mr. Muiderstr.

Hortus Botanicus

Plantage Kerklaan

Entrepotdok

ARTIS ZOO

Nieuwe Keizersgracht

Plantage Muidergracht

Plantage Middenlaan

Sarphatistraat

Singelgracht

Mauritskade

Hermitage Amsterdam

Kerkstraat

Magere Brug

Nieuwe Prinsengracht

Amstel

Nieuwe Weesperstraat

Nieuwe Achtergracht

Amstel-sluizen

Weesper-plein straat

Singelgracht

Tropen-museum

Weesperplein **M**

Mauritskade

Limeausstraat

Sarphati-

Hoge-sluis

Boerhaave-plein

Sajet-plein

's-Gravesande-str.

OOSTERPARK

Weesperzijde

Wibautstraat

's-Gravesande-plein

Oosterpark

Kastanje-plein

Toronto Brug

River Amsteldijk

Ruyschstr.

Eiken-plein

Blasiusstr.

Eerste Oosterparkstr.

Beuken-plein

ⓘ Information

✉ Main Post Office

Ⓜ Metro

0 ___ 200 yds
0 ___ 200 m

Holland's history and culture are inextricably linked to the sea, as you'll discover for yourself on a maritime tour of Amsterdam. This tour takes you to one of the country's best maritime museums, guides you across the river on a ferry, and then lets you peek inside a houseboat. START: **Bus no. 22, 42, or 43 to Kattenburgerplein.**

A boy gets a close-up look at a cannon at the Maritime Museum.

1 ★★ kids **Scheepvaartmuseum (Maritime Museum).** This gem of a museum overlooks the busy harbor. Sadly, it is closed for major renovations until mid-2010, making it an exterior-view-only attraction for most of the lifetime of this edition of *Amsterdam Day by Day.* For those who make it inside the grand museum, gems include the Royal Barge, used by the monarchy from 1818 to 1982. The rooms are filled with boats and ship models; paintings

and prints of ships, seascapes, navigational instruments, cannons and other weaponry; old maps and charts; and important historical papers. ⏱ *3 hr. (when the museum reopens). Kattenburgerplein 1 (in the Eastern Dock).* ☎ *020/523-2222. www.scheepvaartmuseum.nl. The following prices and hours were current when the museum was last open and may change. Admission 7.50€ adults, 4€ kids 6–17. Tues–Sat 10am–5pm (also Mon during school vacations); Sun noon–5pm. Bus: 22 or 32 to Kattenburgerplein.*

2 ★★ kids **Passenger Terminal Amsterdam.** It can be interesting to visit this ultramodern facility just east of Centraal Station when a giant oceangoing cruise liner is tied up at the dock on the IJ ship channel. At other times you might have to make do with a Rhine River cruise boat down from Switzerland or Germany—still interesting but not in

The merchant ship Amsterdam.

The Houseboat Museum.

the same size league. The neighboring building on the wharf is the shiny glass concert hall Muziekgebouw aan 't IJ (p 117). ⏱ *30 min. Piet Heinkade 27.* ☎ *020/509-1000. www.ptamsterdam.nl. Open when a cruise ship is moored. Free admission. Tram: 25 or 26.*

❸ ★★ kids Crossing the IJ waterway to Amsterdam-Noord. Take this free ferry ride across to the north bank of the IJ channel to see the city and its numerous boats up close. From the dock at Waterplein West, behind Centraal Station, ferries depart every 10 to 15 minutes. ⏱ *5–10-min. crossing.*

❹ ★ kids Wilhelmina-Dok. With its fantastic glass-walled terrace right on the river, this fun cafe-restaurant boasts incredible views of the boats and the cruise-ship terminal on the south shore. Organic salads and delicious sandwiches are the specialties here; if you're eager to continue your maritime experience with a seafood dish, the grilled swordfish with saffron rice is your best bet. *Nordwal 1 (at IJplein).* ☎ *020/632-3701. $$.*

❺ ★ kids Houseboat Museum. Take the ferry back to Centraal Station and jump on the tram to get to this houseboat moored on the edge of the Jordaan. Over 2,400 private houseboats float peacefully on the canals of Amsterdam; this museum gives you an intriguing look inside a particularly well-preserved example. Inside the *Hendrika Maria,* a former commercial sailing vessel built in 1914, you can visit the original deckhouse where the skipper and his family lived. The cupboard bed and the comfortable living quarters are yours to explore. Kids will enjoy the small play area devoted to them. There are plenty of interesting photographs and books relating to houseboats. ⏱ *30 min. Opposite Prinsengracht 296 (near Elandsgracht).* ☎ *020/427-0750. www. houseboatmuseum.nl. Admission 3.25€ adults, 2.50€ kids under 152cm (60 in.). Mar–Oct Tues–Sun 11am–5pm; Nov–Feb Fri–Sun 11am–5pm. Closed Jan 1, Apr 30 & Dec 25, 26 & 27. Tram: 13, 14, or 17 to Westermarkt.*

Alternative Amsterdam

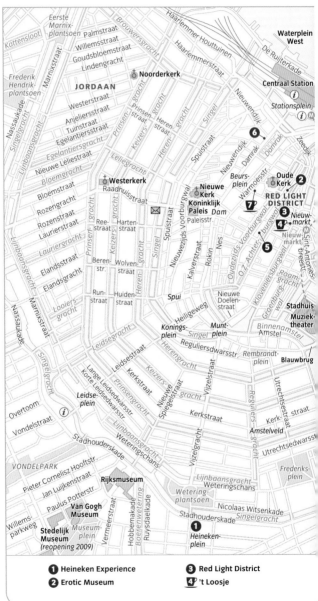

1 Heineken Experience
2 Erotic Museum
3 Red Light District
4 't Loosje

NOORD

Het IJ

Het IJ

| 0 | 200 yds |
| 0 | 200 m |

(i) Information
⊠ Main Post Office
Ⓜ Metro

Sixhaven

IJ-Tunnel

Muziekgebouw
aan 't IJ/
Bimhuis

Passenger Terminal
Amsterdam

Jan Schaefer Brug

JAVA-EILAND

IJhaven

De Ruijterkade

Centraal
Station

Piet Heinkade

Oosterdokskade

Dijksgracht

Komme Waal

Waals

Oosterdok

Binnenkant
eilandsgracht
Oude Waal

Prins Hendrikkade

NEMO

MARINE
ETABLISSEMENT
(NAVAL COMPLEX)

Kattenburgerstr.

Kattenburgervaart

Grote Wittenburgerstraat

Wittenburgervaart

Oude
Nieuwe
Uilenburgerstr.

Schans

Uilenburgergracht

Valkenburgerstraat

Hoogtekadijk

Nieuwe Vaart

Joden-
breestr.

Rapen-
burgerstr.

gracht

Wertheim-
park

Entrepotdok

Waterloo-
plein

Mr.
Visser-
plein

Muiderstr.

Heren

Hortus
Botanicus

Plantage Kerklaan

ARTIS ZOO

Sarphatistraat

Singelgracht

Mauritskade

Ⓜ Waterlooplein

Nieuwe

Nieuwe Keizersgracht

Kerkstraat

Plantage Muidergracht

Plantage Middenlaan

Hermitage
Amsterdam

Magere
Brug

Amstel

Nieuwe
Nieuwe

Weesperstraat

Prinsengracht

Achtergracht

Amstel-
sluizen

Weesper-
plein

straat

Singelgracht

Tropen-
museum

Weesperplein

Sarphati

Mauritskade

Sajet-
plein

's-Gravesande-
str.

Linnaeusstraat

Hoge-
sluis

Wibautstraat

Boerhaave-
plein

's-Gravesande-
plein

OOSTERPARK

Toronto
Brug

Weesperzijde

Ruyschstr.

Oosterpark

Kastanje-
plein

River
Amsteldijk

Blasiusstr.

Eerste Oosterparkstr.

Eerste Oosterparkstr.

Eiken-
plein

Beuken-
plein

❺ Hash Marihuana & Hemp Museum

❻ Sexmuseum Amsterdam

❼ Winston Kingdom

Amsterdam has a reputation for being a wild party town with tolerant attitudes toward many aspects of life. It tolerates the growing and selling of cannabis in small amounts, and Dutch law allows prostitution. The Red Light District is known the world over for its scantily clad women luring customers from behind glass windows. This tour will give you a chance to discover the wilder side of Amsterdam, but not surprisingly, your day may not end until well after midnight. START: Tram 16, 24, or 25 to Stadhouderskade.

1 ★ Heineken Experience. This place is usually a hit with 20-somethings (mostly male), who enjoy the two free beers (and a free Heineken glass as a souvenir) as much as they enjoy the myriad rides and shows. It's a hoot if you just get loose and go with the flow—and you'll learn a few things about beer while you're at it. It's housed inside the former working brewery (built around 1867). The operation moved out of this facility in 1988, but a minibrewery opened in 2008 to afford a miniview of how brewing works. The old fermentation tanks, each capable of holding a million glasses of Heineken, are still here, along with the multistory malt silos, all manner of vintage brewing equipment and implements, and a stable for the strapping Shire horses that pull Heineken's old-world promotional drays. In one amusing attraction, you stand on a moving floor, facing a large video screen, and get to see and feel what it's like to be a Heineken beer bottle careening on a conveyor belt—one of a half million every hour—through a modern Heineken plant. ⏱ *2 hr. Stadhouderskade 78 (at Ferdinand Bolstraat).* ☎ *020/523-9666. www.heineken experience.com. Admission 10€ (includes 2 beers); under 18 not admitted. Tues–Sun 10am–6pm. Closed Jan 1 & Dec 25. Tram: 16, 24, or 25 to Stadhouderskade.*

2 Erotic Museum. Spread over five floors, this wacky place boasts many provocative prints and drawings, including some by John Lennon. More interesting is a re-creation of a red-light alley and an extensively

Copper brewing kettles at the Heineken Experience.

The Erotic Museum is just one of Amsterdam's sex-themed museums.

equipped S&M playroom. Don't miss the X-rated cartoon depicting some of the things Snow White apparently got up to with the Seven Dwarfs that we were never told about as kids! 🕐 45 min. Oudezijds Achterburgwal 54. ☎ 020/623-1834. Admission 5€. Sun–Thurs 11am–1am; Fri–Sat 11am–2am. Tram: 4, 9, 14, 16, 24, or 25 to the Dam.

❸ **Red Light District.** Upon leaving the Erotic Museum, you'll find yourself in the Red Light District. If you take a peek down any of the tiny alleyways, you'll see the prostitutes hanging out behind their windows waiting for customers. Some may be on cellphones, some may be knitting. Many will be in various stages of undress (though never fully naked). If the curtains are closed, then you know that a deal has been . . . consummated. Probably what you'll notice most of all are the throngs of testosterone-driven men circling these tiny alleyways with hungry eyes. It's not dangerous here, just a bit seedy, though you shouldn't take photos at any time; it's best to hide your camera when you stroll here, especially at night. Early evening is the best time to visit, before it gets

crowded but late enough that you can see the red lights reflecting off the canals. 🕐 30 min. Along Oudezijds Achterburgwal and the tiny alleyways that intersect it.

❹ **'t Loosje.** Steps from the Red Light District (toward Nieuwmarkt) is a busy, friendly cafe that was built in 1900. Tiles from that period still ornament the walls. It's a great place to people-watch. Many beers are on tap, and they have a good choice of snacks. Try the Dutch croquettes or *bitterballen* (fried minced-meat-and-potato balls) dipped in hot mustard. Nieuwmarkt 32–34. ☎ 020/627-2635. $.

❺ ★ **Hash Marihuana & Hemp Museum.** Only in Amsterdam, eh? This museum will teach you everything you wanted to know about hash, marijuana, and related products. The museum does not promote drug use; instead it aims to make you better informed. There's a cannabis garden where you can see plants at various stages of development. Some exhibits shed light on

You can find prostitutes waiting for customers around the clock in the Red Light District.

Learn the history of cannabis at the Hash Marihuana & Hemp Museum.

the medicinal use of cannabis and on hemp's past and present-day uses as a natural fiber. ⏱ *1 hr. Oudezijds Achterburgwal 148 (Red Light District).* ☎ *020/623-5961. www.hashmuseum.com. Admission 5.70€ adults, free for kids under 13. Daily 10am–10pm. Closed Jan 1, Apr 30 & Dec 25. Tram: 4, 9, 14, 16, 24, or 25 to the Dam.*

6 Sexmuseum Amsterdam. For more of Amsterdam's wild side, head over to this museum—or "Venustempel," as it dubs itself. More than half a million visitors traipse through here every year to learn more about the history of sex. Teenagers end up giggling quite a bit. "Sex through the ages and cultures" is the theme of one exhibit, which includes such 19th-century erotic objects as a fragment of a Delft blue tile showing a man with an erection playing cards. There's an interesting exhibit about early erotic photography and many erotic prints and drawings and trinkets decorated with naughty pictures. It's open late, so you can come here after dark, before you head out to the club below. ⏱ *1 hr. Damrak 18 (near Centraal Station).* ☎ *020/622-8376. www.sexmuseumamsterdam.com. Admission 3€; under 17 not admitted. Daily 10am–11:30pm. Closed Dec 25. Tram: 1, 2, 4, 5, 9, 13, 16, 17, 24, 25, or 26 to Centraal Station.*

7 ★ Winston Kingdom. End your day at this very happening and very fun venue inside the Winston Hotel at the edge of the Red Light District. You'll find live music, drag shows, singalongs, and other shows every night of the week in this small, intimate space with a very eclectic, live-and-let-live, quintessentially Amsterdam crowd. The dress code is suave, sexy, and glamorous, but basically anything goes as long as you're having a good time. There are light snacks and drinks, and the cover ranges between 5€ and 8€. Things really get going after 10pm. *Winston Hotel, Warmoesstraat 131.* ☎ *020/623-1380. $.* ●

The Sexmuseum, another of Amsterdam's sex-themed museums.

3 The Best
Neighborhood Walks

Golden Age **Canals**

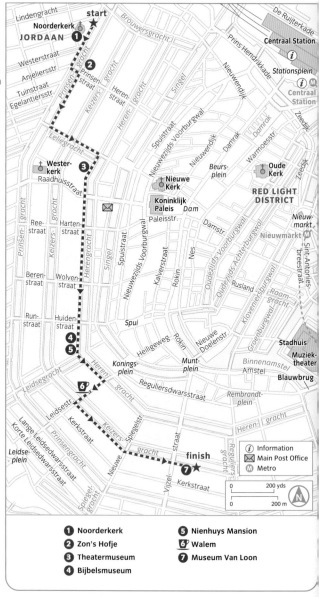

1 Noorderkerk

2 Zon's Hofje

3 Theatermuseum

4 Bijbelsmuseum

5 Nienhuys Mansion

6 Walem

7 Museum Van Loon

Previous page: A woman bikes past canal houses.

Amsterdam's glory days date back to the 17th century, a time known as the "Golden Age." This tour gives you an in-depth view of the brilliant architecture of that time as you pass innumerable canal houses with gables in various styles (bell, step, neck, and variations), as well as a peek into hidden almshouses and courtyards and the opportunity to visit three important museums. START: **Tram no. 1, 2, 5, 13, or 17 to Martelaarsgracht.**

1 ★ **Noorderkerk.** The North Church was the last masterpiece by architect Hendrick de Keyser, the guiding hand behind many of Amsterdam's historic churches. Dating back to 1623, it was built for the poor Calvinist faithful of the Jordaan nearby. It was restored during the 1990s and today has an active congregation. From May to September a classical-music recital takes place here every Saturday at 2pm; admission is 14€. Noordermarkt, the square on which the church is located, hosts a Saturday farmers market with organic products for sale from 10am to 3pm. ⏲ *30 min. Noordermarkt 44–48 (at Prinsengracht).* ☎ *020/626-6436. Free admission. Mon 10:30am–12:30pm; Sat 11am–1pm; Sun services 10am & 7pm.*

2 **Zon's Hofje.** Walk up Prinsengracht to no. 159, where you'll find a hidden *hofje* (almshouse) surrounding a courtyard garden at the end of a long passageway. Almshouses are like cloisters and always have a garden in the middle. They were built by wealthy citizens starting in the 14th century for the old and needy; many were inhabited by pious women. Today, students, seniors, and people who need assisted living reside in almshouses. At Zon's Hofje, the outer door is open from 10am to 5pm Monday through Saturday, and you can walk quietly through the passageway to the courtyard, which belonged to the city's Mennonites. They held meetings in this serene courtyard, which they called De Kleine Zon (the Little Sun). This is a great place for a moment of contemplation, away from the bustle of the city. *Prinsengracht 159–171.*

The interior of the Noorderkerk.

③ ★ Theatermuseum. Back on Prinsengracht, turn left along the picturesque Leliegracht canal, and then turn right onto Herengracht, the ultimate Amsterdam address for flourishing bankers and merchants in the 17th century. At no. 168 is the Theatermuseum, in a building known as the Het Witte Huis (the White House) for its whitish-gray, neoclassical sandstone facade. This graceful house was built in 1638 for Michiel Pauw, who established a short-lived trading colony in America at Hoboken, New Jersey. Dazzling interior ornamentation from around 1730 includes a spiral staircase, intricate stuccowork, and painted ceilings by Jacob de Wit. The museum extends into the flamboyant Bartolotti House (nos. 170–172), built in 1617 for Guillielmo Bartolotti. Bartolotti began life as Willem van den Heuvel and switched to the fancier moniker after he made a bundle in brewing and banking. In the museum you'll find costumes, masks, puppets, photos, miniature theaters, and backdrops. Hands-on exhibits let you create your own stage and sound effects. ⏲ 1 hr.

The Bijbels Museum.

Herengracht 168. ☎ 020/551-3300. www.tin.nl. Admission 4.50€ adults; 2.25€ seniors, students & kids 7–16. Mon–Fri 11am–5pm; Sat–Sun 1–5pm. Closed Jan 1, Apr 30 & Dec 25.

④ Bijbels Museum (Biblical Museum). Stroll down Herengracht, taking in the view of the canals and canal houses with their varied gables. Two of a group of four 1660s houses (nos. 364–370) with delicate neck gables house the Biblical Museum. The houses were designed by architect Philips Vingboons for timber merchant Jacob Cromhout and are known as the Cromhouthuizen or as the "Father, Mother, and Twins." The museum itself features Bibles and things biblical, but its canal-house setting with its elegant stucco decoration, dizzying elliptical staircase, and illuminated ceilings by Jacob de Wit are worth the admission price alone. ⏲ 1 hr. Herengracht 366–368. ☎ 020/624-2436. www.bijbels museum.nl. Admission 7.50€ adults, 4.50€ students, 3.75€ kids 13–17. Mon–Sat 10am–5pm; Sun and holidays 11am–5pm. Closed Jan 1 & Apr 30.

⑤ Nienhuys Mansion. A few steps down Herengracht bring you to this princely residence (at nos. 380–382). Constructed in 1890 for Dutch tobacco merchant Jacob Nienhuys, it now houses the Netherlands Institute for War Documentation (not open to visitors). Across the canal, on the facade of Herengracht 395, a stone cat stalks its prey—a carved mouse on the facade of the neighboring house, no. 397 (it's not easy to see unless you cross over tiny Beulingsluis canal for a close-up look). Herengracht 380–382.

⑥ ★ Walem. Cross elegant Leidsegracht (dug in 1664 for barge traffic) and walk along Leidsestraat to its

Gables 101

Most of Amsterdam's 6,800 landmark buildings have gables. These hide the pitched roofs and demonstrate the architect's vertical showmanship in a city where hefty property taxes and expensive canalfront land encouraged pencil-thin buildings. If you can pick out Amsterdam's various gable styles without developing Sistine Chapel–neck syndrome, you can date the buildings fairly accurately. Of the earliest, triangular wood gables (1250–1550) only two remain, at no. 34 in the Begijnhof and at Zeedijk 1. Later developments in stone on this theme (1600–50) were the pointy spout gable and the step gable, which, as the name suggests, looks like a series of steps. The graceful neck gable (1640–1790) looks like a headless neck, with curlicues on the shoulders.

junction with Keizersgracht. Walem, with its interior designed by Philippe Starck, is a trendy cafe-restaurant with two fine terraces (one outside beside the canal and the other at the rear in a sheltered and quiet garden patio). The home-smoked-salmon sandwich on fresh farm bread with chives, crème fraîche, and cucumbers is exquisite. *Keizersgracht 449.* ☎ *020/625-3544. $$.*

7 ★ Museum Van Loon.
Continue down Keizersgracht to yet another magnificent canal house, this one dating back to 1672. Its first occupant was the artist Ferdinand Bol, a student of Rembrandt. The elegant home was owned by the Van Loon family from 1884 to 1945. On its walls hang more than 80 family portraits, including those of Willem van Loon, one of the founders of the Dutch United East India Company. A marble staircase with an ornately curlicued brass balustrade leads up through the house, connecting restored period rooms that are filled with richly decorated paneling, stuccowork,

mirrors, fireplaces, furnishings, porcelain, medallions, chandeliers, rugs, and more. Be sure to look out into the garden at the carefully tended hedges and the coach house modeled on a Greek temple. ⏱ *1 hr. Keizersgracht 672.* ☎ *020/624-5255. www.museumvanloon.nl. Admission 6€ adults, 4€ students & kids 6–18. Wed–Mon 11am–5pm.*

A room inside the richly decorated Museum Van Loon.

The Jordaan

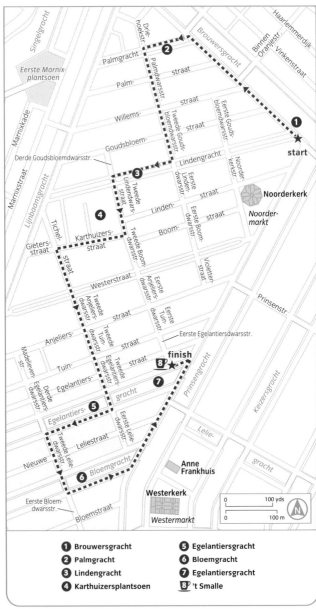

1. Brouwersgracht
2. Palmgracht
3. Lindengracht
4. Karthuizersplantsoen
5. Egelantiersgracht
6. Bloemgracht
7. Egelantiersgracht
8. 't Smalle

The Jordaan is one of Amsterdam's most interesting neighborhoods, where many of the city's more successful artists, intellectuals, and slightly older yuppies reside. Among the district's charms are tiny canals with many bridges, and several of the delightful, centuries-old almshouses called hofjes. If you enter these courtyards, tread softly—people live here. This walk can be taken at any time, though the late afternoon on a warm day would be best so you can end at a canalside cafe. START: **Tram no. 1, 2, 4, 5, 9, 16, 24, 25, or 26 to Centraal Station, and then a 10-minute walk to Brouwersgracht.**

1 ★ Brouwersgracht. Stroll along this old houseboat-lined canal and cross Lindengracht. You'll pass a bronze sculpture from 1979 of Jordaan schoolchild Kees de Jongen, a popular fictional character of Dutch writer Theo Thijssen (1879–1943). Keep going until you cross Willemstraat, and then look across the water for a wide view of the modern De Blauwe Burgt apartment block (you can cross over on the Oranjebrug bridge for a close-up look). It's a good example of the new architecture mixed with the old.

2 Palmgracht. Turn left onto this tree-shaded street, which was once a canal. The house at nos. 28–38 hides a small cobblestone courtyard garden behind an orange door that's the entrance to the Raepenhofje, an almshouse from 1648. If

you're lucky, the door will be open and you can peek into the courtyard. *Palmgracht 28–38.*

3 Lindengracht. Turn left on Palmdwarsstraat and cross over Willemstraat (which used to be a canal known as Goudsbloemgracht) onto Tweede Goudsbloemdwarsstraat. Cross over Goudsbloemstraat to Lindengracht. This was once the Jordaan's most important canal (since filled in) and is now the scene of a lively Saturday street market. The 15 small houses (originally there were 19) of the pretty Suyckerhoff Hofje, at Lindengracht 149–163, were built in 1670 as a refuge for Protestant widows and for women of good moral standing and a "tranquil character," who had been abandoned by their husbands. The door may be closed, but you can generally open it during

One of Brouwersgracht's houseboats.

One of Egelantiersgracht's cafes.

daylight hours and walk along the narrow entrance corridor to a courtyard garden filled with flowers and plants. *Lindengracht 149–163.*

④ Karthuizersplantsoen. From Lindengracht, turn left onto Tweede Lindendwarsstraat. Nothing is left of the Carthusian monastery from 1394 that once stretched from here to Lijnbaansgracht (the monastery was destroyed in the 1570s). A playground marks the spot where its cemetery stood. At Karthuizersstraat 11–19 is a row of neck-gabled houses from 1737, named after the four seasons: Lente, Zomer, Herfst, and Winter (spring, summer, fall,

winter). Next door (despite the unusual numbering), at nos. 69–191, is the Huyszitten-Weduwenhof, which dates from 1650 and used to shelter poor widows. Today students live in these houses, which surround a large interior courtyard. *Karthuizersstraat 11–19.*

⑤ ★ Egelantiersgracht. Hang a left on Tichelstraat to reach Egelantiersgracht. As you make your way here, you'll notice the tall spire of the Westerkerk. Named for the eglantine rose, or sweetbrier, Egelantiersgracht is one of the city's most picturesque and tranquil small canals and is lined with 17th- and 18th-century houses. This is where successful Amsterdam artisans lived in the 17th century. If the door is open, take a peek into the Andrieshofje at nos. 107–145. Cattle farmer Ivo Gerrittsszoon financed this almshouse of 36 houses, which was completed in 1617 and remodeled in 1884. A corridor decorated with Delft blue tiles leads up to a small courtyard with a manicured garden. *Egelantiersgracht 107–145.*

⑥ Bloemgracht. The grandest of the Jordaan canals, Bloemgracht originally was home to workers who produced dyes and paints. The three step-gabled houses at nos. 87–91 were built in 1642 by architect

Bloemgracht.

Egelantiersgracht.

Hendrick de Keyser and now house a foundation established to preserve his work. Their carved gable stones represent a townsman, a country-man, and a seaman. Nos. 77 and 81 are two former sugar refineries from 1752 and 1763.

7 ★ **Egelantiersgracht.** Make a left on Prinsengracht and you'll find yourself back at Egelantiersgracht. The hardware store at nos. 2–6, at the corner of Prinsengracht, is a fine example of an Amsterdam School of Architecture design from 1917. Its intricate brickwork and cast-iron ornaments were influenced by Art Nouveau. To the left of the store, at no. 8, a step-gabled house from 1649 is decorated with sandstone ornaments and gable stones that depict St. Willibrord and a brewer.

8 ★ **'t Smalle.** With its waterside terrace, this cafe is one of the best in the Jordaan for a drink and a typi-cal Dutch snack of bitterballen (fried minced-meat-and-potato balls), chunks of Gouda dipped in mustard, or homemade pea soup. *Egelantiersgracht 12.* ☎ *020/623-9617. $.*

Walking Tour Tips

Allow between 2 and 2½ hours for walking around the Jordaan. If you want to visit one of this neighborhood's lively markets, go either on a Monday morning or on Saturday. On Monday, there's a flea market on Noordermarkt and a textiles market on Westerstraat where you find, among other items, fabrics, and secondhand cloth-ing. On Saturday, Noordermarkt hosts a bird market and a farmers market that has organically grown produce, and Lindengracht has a general street market. For more on shopping in this area, see chapter 4.

56

The Best Neighborhood Walks

The Jewish Quarter

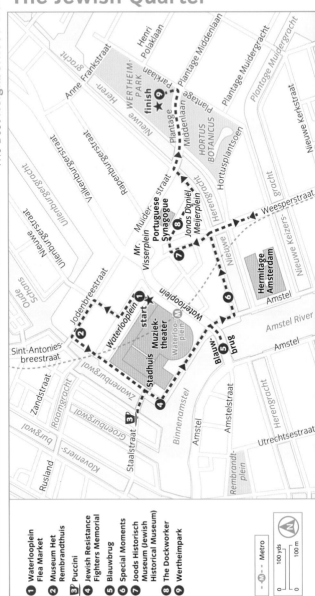

1 Waterlooplein Flea Market
2 Museum Het Rembrandthuis
3 Puccini
4 Jewish Resistance Fighters Memorial
5 Blauwbrug
6 Special Moments
7 Joods Historisch Museum (Jewish Historical Museum)
8 The Dockworker
9 Wertheimpark

This historical area, just to the east of the Old Center, used to be Amsterdam's main Jewish neighborhood. It has changed almost beyond recognition since World War II, but there remain mementos and memorials of Amsterdam's once-thriving Jewish community. It's a great area for a stroll, starting with the city's most popular flea market near the Muziektheater (the home of the Netherlands Opera and Ballet) and Town Hall, and ending with the rich Jewish Historical Museum. START: **Tram no. 9 or 14 to Waterlooplein.**

1 ★ Waterlooplein Flea Market. The most popular flea market in Amsterdam sells everything from sweaters, hats, and gloves to CDs, books, and faux Rembrandt paintings. You'll also find stalls selling raw herring and herring sandwiches. If you're feeling adventurous, try a local favorite: a herring sandwich with pickles and raw onion. In the passageway between the Muziektheater and the Town Hall, you'll see three acrylic columns filled with water. This is the NAP, Normaal Amsterdams Peil (Normal Amsterdam Level), a fixed point against which measurements of sea level are made. The NAP is the standard for altitude measurements in Europe. The first two columns show the current sea level at Vlissingen (a city at the mouth of the Scheldt estuary in the southwestern part of the country) and IJmuiden (a seaport at the mouth of the North Sea Canal, west of Amsterdam); the third, 4.6m (15 ft.) above your head, shows the high-water mark during the disastrous floods in Zeeland in 1953. *Waterlooplein. Market open Mon–Sat 10am–5pm.*

Waterlooplein Flea Market.

The interior of the Rembrandt House.

❷ ★★ Museum Het Rembrandthuis. Continue down on Waterlooplein to the end and turn left on Jodenbreestraat. At nos. 4–6 you'll find Rembrandt's house, now a fabulously preserved museum. Although Rembrandt was not Jewish, he often painted portraits of his Jewish friends and neighbors. A visit to the museum will not only give you an insight into the artist's life and work but will also give you an opportunity to see the interior and furnishings of a 17th-century home in this area. The house was constructed in 1606; Rembrandt bought it in 1639 and lived here until he went bankrupt in 1658. See p 19, **❼**.

❸ Puccini. Just across the bridge to Staalstraat (keep the water to your right when leaving the Rembrandt House), you'll find this delightful bakery and cafe that makes luscious pastries, tarts, and sandwiches. Try one of the fresh berry pies if it's summer, or a pear or apple pie if it's winter. *Staalstraat 17.* ☎ *020/427-8341. $.*

❹ Jewish Resistance Fighters Memorial. Retrace your steps across the bridge and turn right to see this striking black marble monument. It's dedicated to those Jews who tried to resist Nazi oppression and to the people who helped them. *Waterlooplein.*

❺ Blauwbrug (Blue Bridge). Turn left at the monument (the Amstel River will be to your right) and walk toward this notable bridge with its blue lanterns. The cast-iron bridge, inspired by Paris's Pont Alexandre III and opened in 1884, is named after a 16th-century timber bridge painted blue after the 1578 Protestant takeover. Amsterdam's great Impressionist artist George Hendrik Breitner (1857– 1923) painted a picture of this bridge in the 1880s. *Amstelstraat– Waterlooplein.*

❻ Special Moments. Don't cross the Blauwbrug; instead, continue straight ahead, keeping the river to your right. Go left on Nieuwe Herengracht. At no. 33 you'll see the building that was once a Portuguese Jewish home for seniors (they had room for only 10 people and they had their own synagogue inside). Walk to the end of the street and turn right across Vaz Diasbrug. Take a look back down the canal as you cross the bridge and you'll find a picture-perfect view of canal houses and houseboats that's very typically Amsterdam. Continue along this road (Weesperstraat) until you reach a small garden. Here, you'll find a monument to Dutch people who protected their Jewish compatriots during World War II. The memorial, from 1950, takes the shape of a white limestone altar and has reliefs of mourning men, women, and children. This is a great garden for a moment of contemplation.

⑦ ★★ Joods Historisch Museum (Jewish Historical Museum). Head back up Weesperstraat and turn left to reach this museum. The building once housed four synagogues built by Jewish refugees from Germany and Poland in the 17th and 18th centuries. They survived the Nazi occupation of Amsterdam during World War II more or less intact, were sold to the city in 1955, and then stood empty for many years. In 1987 they became home to an impressive collection of Jewish paintings and decorative and ceremonial objects that were looted during the war. In addition to admiring the beauty of the buildings themselves (which include the oldest public synagogue in Europe), you can enjoy some short documentaries about Jewish customs and traditions such as bar mitzvahs and funerals. The museum regularly holds special screenings of features and documentaries pertaining to Jewish history and culture. ⓘ 1½ hr. Nieuwe Amstelstraat 1. ☎ 020/531-0310. www.jhm.nl. Admission 7.50€ adults, 4.50€ seniors & students, 3€ kids 13–17. Fri–Wed 11am–5pm, Thurs 11am–9pm; Jan 1 noon–5pm. Closed Jewish New Year (2 days) & Yom Kippur.

⑧ The Dockworker. Jonas Daniël Meijerplein is where many Jews were forced to wait for their deportation to concentration camps. This bronze statue by Mari Andriessen was erected in 1952 in commemoration of the 1941 February strike by the workers of Amsterdam to protest the deportation of the city's Jewish population. The strike, one of the biggest collective actions in all of occupied Europe against the Nazi persecution, was violently suppressed. *Jonas Daniël Meijerplein).*

A menorah at the Jewish Historical Museum.

⑨ Wertheim Park. This small park—really it's more like a large garden—is a good place for a rest, on benches around its rim. At the park's center is a memorial by sculptor Jan Wolkers to the victims of Auschwitz. Six large "broken" mirrors laid flat on the ground reflect a shattered sky and cover a buried urn containing ashes of the dead from the concentration camp. NOOIT MEER AUSCHWITZ (NEVER AGAIN AUSCHWITZ) reads the dedication. An information board lists in impersonal round numbers some of the gruesome statistics of the Holocaust: Of 140,000 members of Holland's Jewish community, 107,000 were deported to concentration camps, and just 5,200 returned; of the 95,000 sent to Auschwitz and Sobibor, fewer than 500 survived. One of those who perished (at Bergen-Belsen) was Anne Frank, who has a street named after her at the far end of the park. *Plantage Middenlaan.*

The Old Center

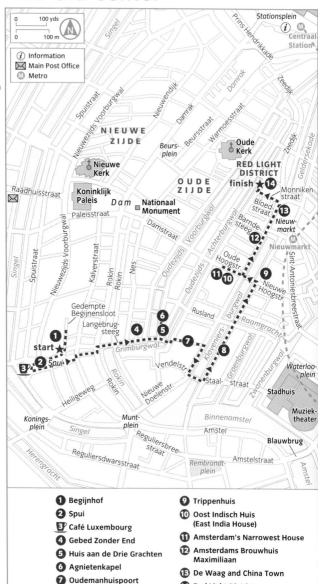

0 100 yds
0 100 m

ⓘ Information
✉ Main Post Office
Ⓜ Metro

1 Begijnhof
2 Spui
3 Café Luxembourg
4 Gebed Zonder End
5 Huis aan de Drie Grachten
6 Agnietenkapel
7 Oudemanhuispoort
8 Poppenhuis
9 Trippenhuis
10 Oost Indisch Huis (East India House)
11 Amsterdam's Narrowest House
12 Amsterdams Brouwhuis Maximiliaan
13 De Waag and China Town
14 Red Light District

This walk takes you into the heart of the oldest part of the city, where you can see the oldest remaining structure in Amsterdam as well as the city's narrowest house. This is the core of Amsterdam, the epicenter from which the city expanded into other directions. Take this walk in the afternoon if you can and leave yourself some time to people-watch at one of the city's notable cafes. The walk ends near the Red Light District. START: **Begijnhof (tram no. 1, 2, 4, 5, 9, 14, 16, 24, or 25 to Spui).**

❶ ★★ **Begijnhof.** This cluster of small homes around a leafy garden courtyard is the best place to appreciate the history of old Amsterdam. No. 34 is the city's oldest house, built in 1425 as a home for devout women. It is one of only two timber houses remaining in the city. Amsterdam was a destination for religious pilgrims and an important Catholic center. The Begijnhof (a cloister) offered women the option to live without a husband and children, and without becoming a nun, at a time when there was little in the way of alternatives. Originally it was surrounded by water, with access via a bridge over the Begijnensloot canal (since filled in). It remained in operation even after the 1578 changeover of the city from Catholicism to Protestantism. The last begijn died in 1971, but you can still pay homage to these pious women by pausing for a moment at the small flower-planed mound that lies just at the center garden's edge, across from the Engelse Kerk (English Church), which dates back to 1607. Opposite the front of the church, at no. 30, is the Begijnhofkapel, a secret Catholic chapel from 1671 that's still in use today. The houses are now a home for seniors. 🕘 *30 min. Spui & Gedempte Begijnensloot. No phone. Free admission. Daily 9am–7pm.*

The Begijnhof garden.

Spui.

2 Spui. This square is both elegant and animated. At its south end is a statue of a small boy, Het Lieverdje (The Little Darling), who is supposed to represent a typical Amsterdam child. Across the street, at no. 21, is the Maagdenhuis, the main downtown building of the University of Amsterdam. *Spui.*

3 ★ Café Luxembourg. The New York Times named this bohemian place "one of the world's greatest cafes." Though I wouldn't go that far, it's certainly a grand cafe. The sidewalk tables are a wonderful place to people-watch in summer while enjoying a toasted Gouda sandwich and a cup of strong Dutch coffee (ideally not served with the typical syrupy-sweet condensed milk). *Spuistraat 24.* ☎ *020/620-6264.* $$.

4 Gebed Zonder End. This tiny alleyway is located in the district known as De Wallen (The Walls), and its name, which means "prayer without end," comes from the convents that used to be here. Legend has it that you could always hear

the murmur of prayers from behind the walls. You are in the heart of Old Amsterdam here—the streets are narrow and a bit confusing. *To reach the alleyway, go to the end of Spui and cross Rokin and Nes, walking along Lange Brugsteeg to Grimburgwal.*

5 Huis aan de Drie Grachten (House on the Three Canals). Continue on Grimburgwal and cross Oudezijds Voorburgwal and Oudezijds Achterburgwal. Between these two canals you'll find this restored handsome redbrick, step-gabled, Dutch Renaissance house from 1609, with red-painted wooden shutters. *Oudezijds Voorburgwal 249.*

6 Agnietenkapel. Stroll a short way along Oudezijds Voorburgwal canal to no. 231, where you'll spot an elaborately ornamental gateway from 1571. This was the chapel of the St. Agnes Convent until the Protestant takeover of Amsterdam. It later formed part of the Athenaeum Illustre, the city's first university, and now houses the university museum, which is not very interesting unless there's a special exhibit. *Oudezijds Voorburgwal 231.*

Detail of the portal at Agnietenkapel.

De Waag.

7 Oudemanhuispoort. Backtrack to the House on the Three Canals and cross the bridge to the far side of Oudezijds Achterburgwal. You'll pass the Gasthuis, once a hospital and now part of the University of Amsterdam campus, and turn right into a dimly lit arcade, the Oudemanhuispoort, that hosts a secondhand-book market Monday to Saturday 10:30am to 6pm. If you're interested, browse around here for a few minutes. In the middle of the arcade, on the left, you'll see a doorway leading to a courtyard garden with a statue of Minerva. It's a lovely place for a few quiet minutes of peace. *Off Grimburgwal.*

8 Poppenhuis. Turn right on Kloveniersburgwal and cross over the canal and go left to reach this handsome classical mansion built in 1642 for Joan Poppen, a dissolute grandson and heir to a rich German merchant. The youth hostel next door at no. 97 was originally a home for retired sea captains. *Kloveniersburgwal 95.*

9 Trippenhuis. Nearby you'll see this house built between 1660 and 1664 for the Trip brothers, who were arms dealers (which explains the martial images and emblems dotted about the house). Originally there were two houses behind a single classical facade, but the two have since been joined. It now houses the Royal Netherlands Academy of Science and is not open for visitors. *Kloveniersburgwal 29.*

10 Oost-Indisch Huis (East India House). Backtrack to the canal bridge and cross over to Oude Hoogstraat, where you can enter this impressive 1606 building via a courtyard on the left side of the street. Once the headquarters of the Vereenigde Oostindische Compagnie, or V.O.C. (United East India Company), the house now belongs to the University of Amsterdam. It's not officially open for visits, but you can stroll into the courtyard and through the doors to take a peek at the hallways hung with paintings of the 17th-century Dutch trading settlement of Batavia (now Jakarta, Indonesia). *Oude Hoogstraat 24.*

11 Amsterdam's Narrowest House. Next door, at Oude Hoogstraat 22, is the city's narrowest house, just 2m (6½ ft.) wide.

Shopping at De Bijenkorf

After all this history you may be eager to return to the modern age—and what better way than through some rampant consumerism?

De Bijenkorf (p 72) is Amsterdam's best department store, selling a terrific variety of goods. If you forgot something at home, you can probably find a replacement here.

De Bijenkorf.

Backtrack to Kloveniersburgwal and go left. At no. 26 you'll see another narrow house, the Klein Trippenhuis, the house of the Trip brothers' coachman (p 28, ③). A few doors down, at nos. 10–12, is the drugstore Jacob Hooy & Co., which has been dispensing medicinal relief since 1743.

⑫ Amsterdams Brouwhuis Maximiliaan. This is the city's smallest brewery, in a surviving part of the 16th-century Bethaniën-klooster (Bethanien Convent). It produces 10 different beers and serves them from copper vats. The nuns who once brewed their own beer here have long since departed, but their beer-making tradition continues in this brewery, which has a rustic but chic wood-floored bar and restaurant attached. There are beers to suit all tastes here, from ale to red to dark. The menu includes many dishes with beer as an ingredient. *Kloveniersburgwal 6–8.*

⑬ De Waag (Weigh House) & Chinatown. Kloveniersburgwal ends at Nieuwmarkt, a large square where you'll easily spot the massive edifice that was once one of the city's medieval gates, and later the Weigh House and guild offices. Nieuwmarkt is the gateway to both the city's Chinatown and Red Light District. Small, family-run Chinese restaurants abound on the square and the little streets leading away from it. *See p 28, ①.*

⑭ Red Light District. This is a good chance to tour the Red Light District (p 14, ⑧). To do that, take Monnickenstraat to Oudezijds Achterburgwal and turn right, and you'll find many windows that frame prostitutes waiting for customers. When you're finished strolling, you can catch the Metro from Nieuwmarkt station or walk the 10 minutes to Centraal Station or the Dam to catch a tram. ●

Shopping **Best Bets**

Best **Wine Store**
★ De Ware Jacob, *Herenstraat 41 (p 76)*

Best **Antiques**
★ Premsela & Hamburger, *Pieter Cornelisz Hooftstraat (p 70)*

Best **Delftware**
★★ Jorrit Heinen, *Prinsengracht 440 (p 72)*

Best **English-Language Bookstores**
★ American Book Center, *Spui 12 (p 70);* and Evenaar, *Singel 348 (p 70)*

Best **Place to Score Castro's Favorite Stogies**
★ P.G.C. Hajenius, *Rokin 92–96 (p 71)*

Best **Place to Shop for Diamonds**
★★ Gassan Diamonds, *Nieuwe Uilenburgerstraat 173–175 (p 74)*

Best **Place to Pick Up Authentic Hunks of Gouda**
★ De Kaaskamer, *Runstraat 7 (p 71)*

Best **Dutch Designer Shoes**
★★ Jan Jansen, *Roelof Hartstraat 16 (p 75)*

Best **Street Market**
★★ Albert Cuypmarkt, *Albert Cuypstraat (p 76)*

Best **Place to Provision for Romance**
E. Kramer Candle Shop, *Reestraat 20 (p 71)*

Best **Place to Stop and Smell the Flowers**
★ Bloemenmarkt (Flower Market), *along the Singel by Muntplein (p 76)*

Best **Place to Shop for Picnic Provisions**
★ Boerenmarkt (Farmers Market), *Noordermarkt (p 76)*

Best **Places to Shop for Gifts for Friends Back Home**
Victoria Gifts, *Prins Hendrikkade 47 (p 74);* and Lush, *Kalverstraat 98 (p 75)*

Best **Department Store**
★★ Metz&Co, *Leidsestraat 34–36 (p 72)*

Best **Designer Boutique for Men, Women & Teens**
★ Azzurro Due, *Pieter Cornelisz Hooftstraat 138 (p 72)*

Best **Unusual Kids' Toys**
Tinkerbell, *Spiegelgracht 10–12 (p 75)*

Best **Designer Goods at Discount Prices**
★ Megazino, *Rozengracht 207–213 (p 73)*

Best **Designer Clothing for Kids**
Oilily, *Pieter Cornelisz Hooftstraat 131–133 (p 75)*

Previous page: An exquisite Delft vase could make an excellent souvenir.
This page: The Albert Cuypmarkt and the Bloemenmarkt are both good places to pick up some fresh blooms.

Museum District **Shopping**

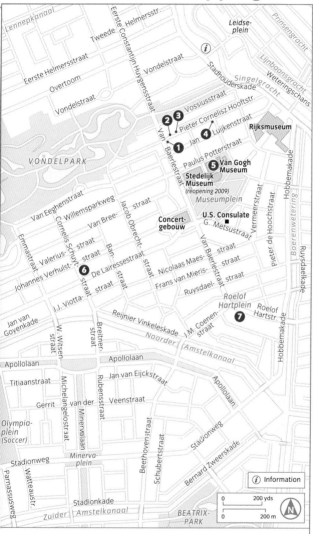

Azzurro Due 2

Carla V 6

Cartier 3

Jan Jansen 7

Louis Vuitton 4

Oilily 1

Van Gogh Museum
  Gift Shop 5

Central Amsterdam **Shopping**

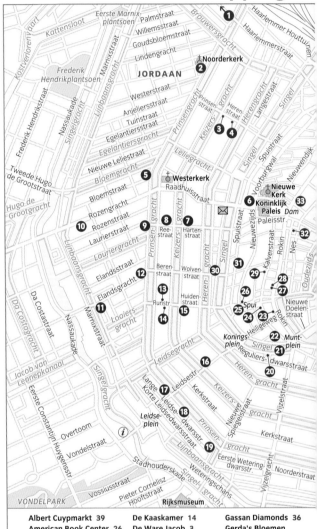

Albert Cuypmarkt 39	De Kaaskamer 14	Gassan Diamonds 36
American Book Center 26	De Ware Jacob 3	Gerda's Bloemen
Betsy Palmer 32	E. Kramer	& Planten 13
Bloemenmarkt 21	Candle Shop 8	Gort 4
Bloomings 1	Episode 37	HEMA 22
Boerenmarkt 2	Evenaar 30	Intermale 31
De Bijenkorf 33	Galleria d'Arte	Jorrit Heinen 17
De Condomerie 35	Rinascimento 5	

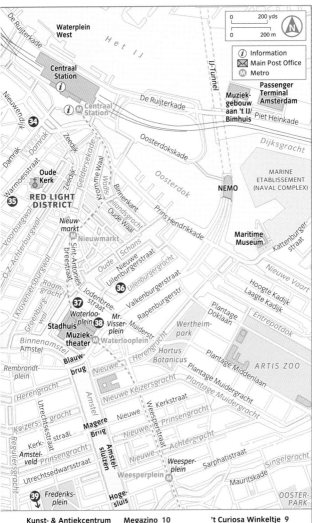

Kunst- & Antiekcentrum
  De Looier 11
La Savonnerie 12
Lush 29
Magic Mushroom
  Gallery 20
Magna Plaza 6
Mathieu Hart 23

Megazino 10
Metz&Co 16
Miauw 7
P.G.C. Hajenius 28
Premsela &
  Hamburger 27
Smokiana 18
Spui Kunstmarkt 25

't Curiosa Winkeltje 9
Tinkerbell 19
Van Ravenstein 15
Victoria Gifts 34
Waterlooplein
  Flea Market 38
Waterstone's 24

Amsterdam Shopping A to Z

Art & Antiques

Mathieu Hart OLD CENTER
Since 1878 this refined store has been selling color etchings of Dutch cities, along with rare old prints, 18th-century delftware, and grandfather clocks. *Rokin 122.* ☎ *020/623-1658. www.hartantiques.com. AE, MC, V. Tram: 4, 9, 14, 16, 24, or 25 to Spui. Map p 68.*

★★ Premsela & Hamburger
OLD CENTER Opened in 1823, this fine jewelry and antique silver seller—purveyors to the Dutch court—boasts a great collection of Old Dutch Silver by 17th-century craftsmen. Their workshop designs and repairs jewelry. *Rokin 98.* ☎ *020/627-5454. www. premsela.com. AE, MC, V. Tram: 4, 9, 14, 16, 24, or 25 to Spui. Map p 68.*

An antique Dutch silver teapot.

Van Gogh Museum Gift Shop
MUSEUM DISTRICT One of the best museum gift stores in the city sells everything from imitations of van Gogh's classics to beautiful mugs painted with his famous sunflowers, plus a good selection of art books. *Paulus Potterstraat 7.* ☎ *020/570-5200. www.vangogh museum.nl. AE, MC, V. Tram: 2, 3, 5, or 12 to Van Baerlestraat. Map p 67.*

Books

★ American Book Center OLD CENTER From novels and Frommer's guides to the latest magazines, this large U.S.-style bookstore is extremely well stocked. *Spui 12.* ☎ *020/625-5537. www.abc.nl. AE, DC, MC, V. Tram: 1, 2, or 5 to Spui. Map p 68.*

Evenaar CANAL BELT Specializing in travel literature, this very well-situated bookstore has everything from travel guides and world maps to all sorts of books on armchair travel and anthropology. You can also find antique travel books here. *Singel 348.* ☎ *020/624-6289. www.evenaar.net. AE, MC, V. Tram: 1, 2, or 5 to Spui. Map p 68.*

If you can't afford the real thing, shop for prints, reproductions, art books, and more at the Van Gogh Museum Gift Shop.

You may have a hard time choosing from the hundreds of cheeses for sale at De Kaaskamer.

Intermale OLD CENTER   This large bookstore claims to have the largest collection of books of interest to gay men in Europe. In addition to books, magazines, and greeting cards in English, they stock Dutch and German periodicals. *Spuistraat 251–253.* ☎ *020/625-0009. www. intermale.nl. MC, V. Tram: 1, 2, or 5 to Spui. Map p 68.*

Waterstone's OLD CENTER   This British chain is very well stocked with the latest fiction and nonfiction releases. You'll find lots of hard-covers here, but they have a wide selection of paperbacks as well. *Kalverstraat 152.* ☎ *020/638-3821. www.waterstones.com. AE, DC, MC, V. Tram: 1, 2, 4, 5, 14, 16, 24, or 25 to Spui. Map p 68.*

Candles
E. Kramer Candle Shop CANAL BELT   All kinds of candles are sold here, from elaborately carved melting works of art to outrageously kitschy wax designs. A good place to pick up scented candles and votives if you're planning a romantic evening in your hotel room. *Reestraat 20.* ☎ *020/ 626-5274. MC, V. Tram: 13, 14, or 17 to Westermarkt. Map p 68.*

Cheese
★ **De Kaaskamer** CANAL BELT   Choose from over 300 cheeses at this store (they will vacuum-pack for travelers) including rows and rows of authentic wheels of Gouda stamped with their farm of origin. *Runstraat 7.* ☎ *020/623-3483. MC, V. Tram: 1, 2, or 5 to Spui. Map p 68.*

Cigars
★ **P.G.C. Hajenius** OLD CENTER   This store has been around since 1826, and it's the best place to shop for Cuban cigars—there's an entire room stocked with Havanas. You'll

Most people associate smoking in Amsterdam with marijuana, but cigar lovers can pick up some fine Cubans here.

also find Dutch handmade clay pipes that make good gifts. *Rokin 92–96.* ☎ *020/623-7494. www.hajenius.com. AE, DC, MC, V. Tram: 4, 9, 14, 16, 24, or 25 to Spui. Map p 68.*

Smokiana CANAL BELT   In addition to cigars, Smokiana sells just about every kind of pipe imaginable, from the antique to the exotic to the downright weird. *Prinsengracht 488.* ☎ *020/421-1779. www.pipeshop.nl. MC, V. Tram: 1, 2, or 5 to Prinsengracht. Map p 68.*

Delftware
Galleria d'Arte Rinascimento CANAL BELT   This well-stocked emporium sells hand-painted delftware of every conceivable type from quality-challenged items to the real thing from De Porcelyne Fles, along with multi-colored (and pricey) makkumware porcelain from Tichelaars. *Prinsengracht 170.* ☎ *020/622-7509. www.delft-art-gallery.com. AE, DC, MC, V. Tram: 13, 14, or 17 to Westermarkt. Map p 68.*

A hand-painted Delft tile makes a great gift for friends back home.

★★ Jorrit Heinen CANAL BELT   One of a family-owned group of Amsterdam stores that makes and sells

Magna Plaza's elegant interior.

own-brand porcelain. They are also official dealers of De Porcelyne Fles delftware, Tichelaars makkumware, fine crystal, and other quality gifts. *Prinsengracht 440.* ☎ *020/421-8360. www.jorritheinen.com. MC, V. Tram: 6, 7, or 10 to Spiegelgracht. Map p 68.*

Department Stores
★ De Bijenkorf OLD CENTER   The city's best-known department store sports the largest variety of goods. From handbags to big-screen TVs, it's all here. *Dam 1.* ☎ *0900/0919. www.bijenkorf.nl. AE, DC, MC, V. Tram: 4, 9, 14, 16, 24, or 25 to the Dam. Map p 68.*

HEMA OLD CENTER   This smaller store is a great place to find a cheap item (gloves, hat, socks) or just a toothbrush. You can get mineral water in large bottles here, too. *Kalvertoren, Kalverstraat 212.* ☎ *020/422-8988. www.hema.nl. MC, V. Tram: 4, 9, 14, 16, 24, or 25 to Muntplein. Map p 68.*

★★ Metz&Co CANAL BELT   Founded in 1740, this is Amsterdam's most upscale department store (like a small Harrods), selling everything from beautiful furniture to gourmet kitchenware. Don't miss the rooftop cafe with its fantastic view of the city. *Leidsestraat 34–36.* ☎ *020/520-7020. www.metzandco.com. AE, DC, MC, V. Tram: 1, 2, or 5 to Keizersgracht. Map p 68.*

Fashion
★ Azzurro Due MUSEUM DISTRICT   The ultimate address for finding a pair of designer jeans or that elusive Prada accessory for both men and women. Azzurro Kids is a few doors down at no. 122. Very chic, very trendy. *Pieter Cornelisz*

Hooftstraat 138. ☎ 020/671-9708. www.azzurrofashiongroup.nl. AE, DC, MC, V. Tram: 2, 3, 5, or 12 to Van Baerlestraat. Map p 67.

Carla V MUSEUM DISTRICT Irrepressible Dutch designer Carla van der Vorst owns this posh boutique specializing in custom ladies' leather clothing. Look for coats, skirts, bags, belts, and more. Skinflints should abstain. *Cornelis Schuytstraat 45.* ☎ 020/672-0404. www.carlav.nl. AE, MC, V. Tram: 2 to Cornelis Schuytstraat. Map p 67.

Louis Vuitton MUSEUM DISTRICT Of course, you'll find the usual upmarket suitcases and handbags here that Vuitton is famous for, but you'll also find a good selection of shoes, jewelry, belts, and ties. *Pieter Cornelisz Hooftstraat 65–67.* ☎ 020/575-5775. www.louisvuitton.com. AE, DC, MC, V. Tram: 2, 3, 5, or 12 to Van Baerlestraat. Map p 67.

★ **Megazino** JORDAAN Large for Amsterdam, this designer outlet store sells everything from Armani, Gucci, and Prada to Calvin Klein and Dolce & Gabbana—all at 30% to 50% off the original price. A great place to burn some plastic without breaking the bank. *Rozengracht 207–213.* ☎ 020/330-1031. www.megazino.nl. AE, MC, V. Tram: 13, 14, or 17 to Westermarkt. Map p 68.

★ **Miauw** CANAL BELT This two-room store is owned by one of Amsterdam's renowned designers, Analik. One room is filled with small pieces of clothing for young and skinny women, the other with funky handbags and other accessories designed by local Dutch artists. *Hartenstraat 36.* ☎ 020/422-0561. www.analik.com. AE, MC, V. Tram: 13, 14, or 17 to Westermarkt. Map p 68.

★ **Van Ravenstein** CANAL BELT The latest creations by up-and-coming Dutch and Belgian designers

Shop for all sorts of designer goods at Amsterdam's Louis Vuitton boutique.

such as Victor and Rolf, Martin Margiela, Dirk Bikkembergs, and Bernhard Willhelm are this small fashion boutique's stock-in-trade. In the basement, a collection of last season's discards is on sale. *Keizersgracht 359.* ☎ 020/639-0067. AE, MC, V. Tram: 1, 2, or 5 to Keizersgracht. Map p 68.

Flowers

Bloomings BOS EN LOMMER This friendly neighborhood florist sells expertly arranged flowers and exquisite vases of all shapes and sizes. *Lucellestraat 20.* ☎ 06/2421-3723. www.bloomings-amsterdam.nl. MC, V. Tram: 14 to Egidiusstraat. Map p 68.

Gerda's Bloemen & Planten CANAL BELT One of the most elegant florists in the city boasts a

Metz&Co.

Fresh tulips for sale at one of Amsterdam's many florists.

fantastic selection of exotic flowers and unusual plants artfully arranged and presented. *Runstraat 16.* ☎ *020/ 624-2912. MC, V. Tram: 1, 2, or 5 to Spui. Map p 68.*

Funky Stores

De Condomerie OLD CENTER The "world's first" condom boutique was the start of a whole new protection racket. Handily sited on the edge of the Red Light District, it stocks a vast range of these singular items, in all shapes, sizes, and flavors, from common brands to flashy designer fittings, all but guaranteeing your apparel of choice. *Warmoesstraat 141 (behind De Bijenkorf).* ☎ *020/ 627-4174. www.condomerie.com. AE, MC, V. Tram: 4, 9, 14, 16, 24, or 25 to the Dam. Map p 68.*

Episode WATERLOOPLEIN Jackets, dresses, scarves, belts, funky brooches, boots—you'll find all these and more at this unisex vintage store. Specialties include flamboyant evening gowns and leather jackets, all in pretty good shape and reasonably priced. *Waterlooplein 1.* ☎ *020/ 320-3000. www.episode.eu. MC, V. Tram: 9 or 14 to Waterlooplein. Map p 68.*

Magic Mushroom Gallery CANAL BELT Only in Amsterdam. Everything from "psychoactive mushrooms" to tonics such as

Yohimbe Rush and Horn E that allegedly improve your sex life. *Singel 524.* ☎ *020/422-7845. MC, V. Tram: 4, 9, 14, 16, 24, or 25 to Muntplein. Map p 20.*

kids 't Curiosa Winkeltje CANAL BELT This funky but fun store sells modern versions of old tin cars, colored bottles and glasses, lamps shaped like bananas, and some children's toys from the 1950s. *Prinsengracht 228.* ☎ *020/625-1352. MC, V. Tram: 13, 14, or 17 to Westermarkt. Map p 68.*

Gifts

Victoria Gifts OLD CENTER This small store is great for finding Dutch clocks and other quality gifts at reasonable prices. *Prins Hendrikkade 47.* ☎ *020/427-2051. www.victoria gifts.nl. MC, V. Tram: 1, 2, 4, 5, 9, 13, 16, 17, 24, 25, or 26 to Centraal Station. Map p 68.*

Jewelry

★ **Cartier** MUSEUM DISTRICT If you must have the best, you've come to the right place. You'll find intricately designed jewelry, watches, pens, and other accessories at this quintessential French store. *Pieter Cornelisz Hooftstraat 132–134.* ☎ *020/670-3434. www.cartier.com. AE, DC, MC, V. Tram: 2, 3, 5, or 12 to Van Baerlestraat. Map p 67.*

★★ **Gassan Diamonds** OLD CENTER This undisputed leader of the city's diamond trade is housed in a stunning Amsterdam School–style building. In addition to shopping for diamonds, you can take a tour that shows you how the jewels are cut. *Nieuwe Uilenburgerstraat 173–175.* ☎ *020/622-5333. www.gassan diamonds.com. AE, DC, MC, V. Tram: 9 or 14 to Waterlooplein. Map p 68.*

★ **Gort** CANAL BELT This beautiful little store specializes in unique and innovative jewelry design. If you like modern and minimalist designs, then this place is for you. *Herenstraat 11.* ☎ *020/620-6240. www.juweliergort. nl. MC, V. Tram: 13, 14, or 17 to Westermarkt. Map p 68.*

Kids

kids Oilily MUSEUM DISTRICT Amsterdam's most upscale children's clothing store has been on the fashion scene since 1963 (they now sell some women's clothing, too). They are known for extremely colorful designs of very high quality. *Pieter Cornelisz Hooftstraat 131–133.* ☎ *020/672-3361. www.oilily-world. com. AE, DC, MC, V. Tram: 2, 3, 5, or 12 to Van Baerlestraat. Map p 67.*

kids Tinkerbell CANAL BELT This unique store sells modern versions of old wood toys. Very Dutch. A great place to find an unusual gift for a child. *Spiegelgracht 10–12.* ☎ *020/ 625-8830. www.tinkerbelltoys.nl. MC, V. Tram: 7 or 10 to Spiegelgracht. Map p 68.*

Malls

★★ **Magna Plaza** OLD CENTER Housed in the city's former main post office, a building that dates from 1908, this elegant mall has four floors filled with about 50 specialist stores from the Body Shop to the Gourmet Cheese Shop. *Nieuwezijds*

Gassan Diamonds offers an informative tour in addition to dazzling gems.

Voorburgwal 182. ☎ *020/626-9199. www.magnaplaza.nl. AE, DC, MC, V. Tram: 1, 2, 5, 13, 14, or 17 to the Dam. Map p 68.*

Shoes

★ **Betsy Palmer** OLD CENTER Imelda Marcos would not approve. There are no classic shoes here, but there's an incredible collection of trendy women's footwear, with obscure but fun brands like Sexy Chic, Sunloving Babe, and Serious Partying. *Rokin 9–15.* ☎ *020/422-1040. www.betsypalmer.com. AE, DC, MC, V. Tram: 4, 9, 14, 16, 24, or 25 to the Dam. Map p 68.*

★★ **Jan Jansen** MUSEUM DISTRICT Award-winning Dutch shoe designer Jan Jansen sells his men's and women's footwear in this chic store. You can special-order colors and sizes if you can't find yours—it takes about 3 weeks and they will mail your shoes to you. *Roelof Hartstraat 16.* ☎ *020/ 470-0116. www.janjansenshoes.com. AE, DC, MC, V. Tram: 3, 5, 12, or 24 to Roelof Hartplein. Map p 67.*

Soap

★ **kids La Savonnerie** CANAL BELT Artisanal soaps of all shapes and sizes are on sale here. The soap chess set makes a great gift. You can buy personalized soap and even make your own. Kids should enjoy the animal-shaped soaps. *Prinsengracht 294.* ☎ *020/428 1139. www. savonnerie.nl. MC, V. Tram: 7, 10, or 17 to Elandsgracht. Map p 68.*

Lush OLD CENTER This popular British chain store sells fragrant and fresh handmade soaps in all flavors and sizes. It's a fun place even for just a quick browse (and a sniff), and their attractive gift packaging makes for great souvenir shopping. *Kalverstraat 98.* ☎ *020/330-6376. www.lush.nl. AE, MC, V. Tram: 4, 9, 14, 16, 24, or 25 to Spui. Map p 68.*

Street Markets

★★ Albert Cuypmarkt PIJP

Unofficially referred to as Europe's largest market, this is Amsterdam's liveliest and most-frequented all-purpose street market, stretching for about 1km (½ mile). From fresh herring and Gouda to silk scarves and hand-knitted hats, you'll find it here Monday to Saturday 9am to 6pm. *Albert Cuypstraat.* ☎ *020/678-1678. www.albertcuypmarkt.com. No credit cards. Tram: 16 or 24 to Albert Cuypstraat. Map p 68.*

★ Bloemenmarkt (Flower Market) CANAL BELT

Partly floating on a row of permanently moored barges, and partly set up along the quay, this is Amsterdam's most popular flower market. You'll find everything from fresh-cut flowers and bright plants to rows and rows of tulip bunches. Fresh-cut tulips cost about the same here as they do at flower stands around town, but this is a great place to pick up ready-to-travel packets of tulip bulbs. Open daily 8am to 8pm. *Along the Singel by Muntplein.* ☎ *020/625-8282. No credit cards. Tram: 9, 14, 16, 24, or 25 to Muntplein. Map p 68.*

★ Boerenmarkt (Farmers Market) JORDAAN

Also known as the Bio (or organic) market, the Boerenmarkt caters to the trendy locals who live in the elegant Jordaan neighborhood. A great place to find fresh vegetables, fruit, cheeses, and organic breads for a picnic. Open Saturday 9am to 5pm. *Noordermarkt. No phone. www.boerenmarktamsterdam.nl. No credit cards. Tram: 1, 2, 5, 13, or 17 to Martelaarsgracht. Map p 68.*

Kunst- & Antiekcentrum De Looier (Antiques) JORDAAN

A large indoor antiques market spread throughout several old warehouses. You'll find everything from furniture and old armoires to 19th-century tin toys, Delft tiles, Dutch knickknacks, and antique jewelry. Open Saturday to Thursday 11am to 5pm. *Elandsgracht 109.* ☎ *020/624-9038. www.looier.nl. No credit cards. Tram: 7, 10, or 17 to Elandsgracht. Map p 68.*

Spui Kunstmarkt (Art Market) OLD CENTER

Every Sunday (9am–5pm) from March to December, local artists mount outdoor exhibits here. You may have to wade through a lot of mediocrity, but it's possible to find something special here. *Spui. No phone. No credit cards. Tram: 1, 2, or 5 to Spui. Map p 68.*

Waterlooplein Flea Market WATERLOOPLEIN

This classic Amsterdam street market has everything from bargain-basement souvenirs to antiques, old CDs, leather jackets, and woolen hats. The market is open Monday to Saturday from 10am to 5pm. *Waterlooplein. No phone. No credit cards. Tram: 9 or 14 to Waterlooplein. Map p 68.*

Wine

★ De Ware Jacob CANAL BELT

Since 1970 this small but charming wine store has carried the finest wines from boutique wineries around the world. *Herenstraat 41.* ☎ *020/623-9877. MC, V. Tram: 13, 14, or 17 to Westermarkt. Map p 68.* ●

A food stand at the Albert Cuypmarkt.

5

The Best of the
Outdoors

Strolling in **Vondelpark**

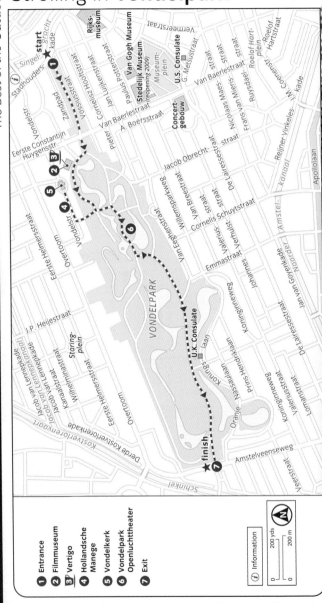

1 Entrance
2 Filmmuseum
3 Vertigo
4 Hollandsche Manege
5 Vondelkerk
6 Vondelpark Openluchttheater
7 Exit

Information

0 ___ 200 yds
0 ___ 200 m

Previous page: Renting a canal bike is an excellent way to delve into Amsterdam's canals.

Amsterdam is not a green city, but Vondelpark provides a tranquil refuge from the bustling crowds. Trees set in an English-style park, manicured rose gardens, ponds, and trails for bikers and in-line skaters abound. Many people use the park to cross from the city's western neighborhoods to its center. Always watch out for speeding bikes as you walk through the park. START: **Tram no. 1, 2, 5, 7, or 10 to Leidseplein.**

❶ ★★ Entrance. Enter the park through the gates closest to Leidseplein, on the corner of Vossiusstraat and Stadhouderskade. This entrance is less than a 5-minute walk from Leidseplein. The sculpture *Maid of Amsterdam,* a symbol of the city, sits over these gates. Keep to your right to avoid the multitudes of zooming bikes (motorized vehicles are not allowed in the park). The park was opened to the public in 1865. J. D. and L. P. Zocher (a father-and-son operation) landscaped what was then a much smaller space, using ponds and pathways to create an English-style garden. Over the years, some 120 different kinds of trees were planted as the park grew to its present size of roughly 44 hectares (109 acres).

❷ ★★ Filmmuseum. From the gates, head south, keeping to the path on your right. After about a 10-minute stroll, you'll see this grand pavilion to your right. It was opened in 1881 as a cafe and restaurant, and was then restored as an international cultural center in 1947. Renovated again in 1991, it is now the country's main film museum. The interior of Amsterdam's first cinema (the Cinema Parisien) was transported here during the last renovations and placed entirely into one of the two theaters. The Art Deco interior alone is worth the price of admission to one of the many screenings that take place here every week. Some films do sell out, so it's not a bad idea to pick up tickets in advance. The two theaters show up to 1,000 films per year, including some English-language films or foreign films with English subtitles. In summer there are occasional free outdoor screenings. (**Note:** The Filmmuseum moves in 2010 to a new location, currently under construction, on the IJ waterfront in Amsterdam-Noord.) *Vondelpark 3.* ☎ *020/589-1400. www.filmmuseum.nl. Admission to exhibits varies; films 7.80€. Museum and library Tues–Fri 10am–5pm, Sat 11am–5pm; box office Mon–Fri 10am–10pm, Sat 6–10pm, Sun 2–10pm. Screenings Mon–Sat 7pm, Sun 3pm & 7pm.*

❸ ★ Vertigo. The Filmmuseum's cafe-restaurant has a popular outdoor terrace with a scenic outlook on the edge of Vondelpark. It serves the usual coffee, sandwiches, and

The Filmmuseum in Vondelpark.

Bicyclists and pedestrians share Vondelpark's paths.

light meals, but there's also an international menu for lunch and dinner. *Vondelpark 3.* ☎ *020/612-3021. $$.*

❹ Hollandsche Manege (Dutch Riding School). When you exit the cafe, stay on the path to the right and you'll see the glorious neoclassical facade of the Dutch Riding School, which was built in 1882. Restored in the 1980s, it still operates as a stable and arena. The building was designed by Adolf Leonard van Gendt (who designed the Concertgebouw) and was modeled after the Spanish Riding School in Vienna. Go inside for a look at its gilded mirrors and molded horses' heads. Be sure to climb up to the balcony for a panoramic view of the arena. You can see the horses perform every Sunday; shows are usually at 3 and 7pm, but call ahead to confirm. You can sign up for a riding lesson (21€ for 1 hr.); contact the school for details. *Vondelstraat 140.* ☎ *020/618-0942. www.dehollandsche manege.nl. Free admission. Tues–Fri 10am–6pm; Sat–Sun 2pm–midnight.*

Freshening Up Vondelpark

The over 10 million visitors that visit Vondelpark every year are seriously impacting the earth. The park was built on peat and now the ground is a good .6m (2 ft.) lower than the surrounding buildings. When it rains, some areas of the park collect water, resulting in large, unwanted ponds. An ambitious renovation project due to end in 2010 is reconnecting some of the older ponds and creating a new drainage system. The landscapers are also planting new varieties of water-absorbing trees and bushes. The work is done in clusters and only small corners of the park at varying seasons of the year are cordoned off—visitors will hardly notice the renovation.

Rollerblading, Anyone?

When you reach the western entrance of the park on Amstelveenseweg, you'll find a rental booth with in-line skates. Rates at De Vondeltuin Rent A Skate (☎ 020/664-5091), are 5€ for the first hour and 2.50€ per subsequent hour, or 15€ for a full day, for both adults and children, and include protective gear. You'll need to bring along an ID and leave a 20€ refundable deposit. It is open daily from 11am to 10pm. If you're game, try joining the 3,000-odd skaters who strap on their 'blades for the regular **Friday Night Skate.** In the summer months, this event begins at 8pm from the Filmmuseum in Vondelpark and takes a route of 15km (9 miles) through the city.

❺ Vondelkerk. Close to the Riding School, you'll see this large church designed by Petrus Josephus Hubertus Cuypers (architect of Centraal Station). It was completed in 1880. A fire in 1904 destroyed its original tower, and a new one was added by the architect's son. In 1985 the church was converted into offices, and sometimes cultural events are held here. *Vondelstraat 120.* ☎ *020/689-7920. Free admission. 1st Wed & 3rd Sun of month noon–4pm.*

❻ ★ kids Vondelpark Openluchttheater (Vondelpark Open-Air Theater). Another few minutes' stroll brings you to this open air venue where summer musical concerts, occasional theater pieces (usually in Dutch), and children's shows (usually in Dutch, but emphasis is on mime and sometimes puppets, so children of all nationalities seem to enjoy the show) are staged free of charge. Performances take place June through August, Thursday to Sunday, at various times. ☎ *020/428-3360. www.openluchttheater.nl. Free admission.*

❼ Exit. By the time you reach the western gates, you'll have walked a little over 1.5km (1 mile). You can exit here and jump on tram no. 1 from Overtoom or no. 2 from Koninginneweg to Centraal Station, or you can head back east, staying to your right to take the path back to the entrance gates close to Leidseplein. The entire loop measures about 3.8km (2.5 miles).

'Blading through Vondelpark is a great way to see the sights and get a little exercise.

Touring Amsterdam by **Canal Bike**

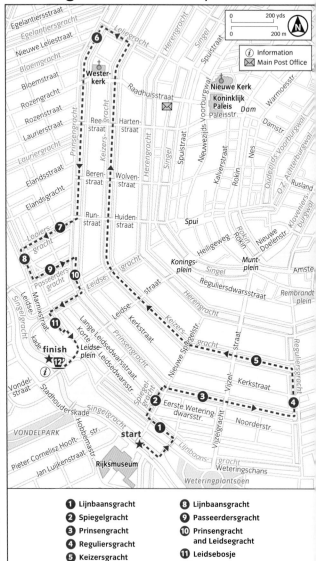

1. Lijnbaansgracht
2. Spiegelgracht
3. Prinsengracht
4. Reguliersgracht
5. Keizersgracht
6. Prinsengracht
7. Looiersgracht
8. Lijnbaansgracht
9. Passeerdersgracht
10. Prinsengracht and Leidsegracht
11. Leidsebosje
12. Café Americain

Canal biking down the city's myriad waterways is an outdoor activity unique to Amsterdam. A lot like pedal boats, these "bikes" let you glide quietly down the canals for a close-up look at houseboats and bridges. You'll also get to admire the many 17th- and 18th-century houses that line the canals from a different vantage point. I don't recommend taking very young kids on the bikes, but older children will likely remember the experience for the rest of their lives. Early on a summer's evening or late on a winter's afternoon is the best time, when the slanting sun hits the buildings and bridges, affording rich opportunities for photos. START: **Tram no. 7 or 10 to Spiegelgracht for the Rijksmuseum mooring.**

1 Lijnbaansgracht. From the Rijksmuseum mooring, take a left on Lijnbaansgracht canal, with its very low bridge and rows of neck-gabled houses. It's a very long canal that provided rope makers (the name translates to "ropewalk") in the 17th century enough space to stretch and twist the ropes they made for the shipbuilding industry in Amsterdam.

2 ★ Spiegelgracht. Turn right onto this short canal lined with antiques shops. There are over 70 specialized antiques dealers in this neighborhood, selling everything from barometers and clocks to brass and copper ornaments. If you choose to stop and have a look, be sure to leave one person in your party with the canal bike—don't leave it unattended.

3 ★★★ Prinsengracht. Turn right onto one of Amsterdam's Golden Age canals. Many of the houses here were built around 1700. Several of them still have their original neck gables.

4 ★ Reguliersgracht. Turn left onto Reguliersgracht. You can spot seven identical arched bridges, perfectly aligned, spanning this canal. These date back to the 17th century. It's a pretty spot for photographs.

5 ★★★ Keizersgracht. Turn left onto Keizersgracht, the city's widest canal at 28m (92 ft.). Some of the houses lining the canal were built as coach houses for the mansions of the prosperous "Golden Bend" stretch of nearby Herengracht. You'll be pedaling for quite some time (30–45 min.)

You can get a close-up view of houseboats and bridges from the seat of a canal bike.

Keizersgracht.

on Keizersgracht as it winds through the edge of the old center and up toward Centraal Station and into the Jordaan. To begin looping back, turn left on tiny Leliegracht and then left on Prinsengracht.

6 ★★★ **Prinsengracht.** You are back on Prinsengracht, but now you are in the heart of the elegant and charming Jordaan neighborhood. The Anne Frank House is here, and the tall spire of the Westerkerk, the largest reformed church in Holland,

Prinsengracht.

will be visible to your right. You'll see many houseboats lining the banks of Prinsengracht, most of them have been here since just after World War II, when the housing shortage forced some people to find alternative dwellings. There are currently some 2,500 houseboats in Amsterdam, and no further permits will be issued for new ones.

7 **Looiersgracht.** Turn right at the "Tanners' Canal"; not surprisingly, this is where leather used to be tanned.

8 **Lijnbaansgracht.** Turn left on the long canal that you pedaled on earlier.

9 ★★★ **Passeerdersgracht.** Turn left here and notice the low railing on the bridge that stops cars from falling into the water. Before the railing was built, cars frequently fell into the canal, and in the 18th century, horses and carriages also tumbled into the water. The railings were not installed until the 1960s—on all 100km (62 miles) of Amsterdam's canals.

10 **Prinsengracht and Leidsegracht.** Turn right and you're on Prinsengracht again. Turn right onto Leidsegracht. Notice the four houses at nos. 72–78, which display four different kinds of gables: No. 72 has a neck gable, 74 a cornice gable, 76 a spout gable, and 78 a step gable (see the box "Gables 101" on p 51 for a primer on gables).

⓫ Leidsebosje. Turn left and you'll spot the large Art Nouveau American Hotel opposite the mooring. You've reached the end! Return your canal bike here.

Café Americain.

⓬ ★★ Café Americain. Overlooking Leidseplein, this turn-of-the-20th-century cafe is a national monument of Dutch Art Nouveau. The infamous spy Mata Hari had her wedding reception here. Don't forget to look up to admire the frosted-glass Tiffany chandeliers. The hamburgers here are especially good, served with thick-cut home fries; there are also plenty of salads and sandwiches to choose from. *In the Amsterdam American Hotel, Leidsekade 97.* ☎ *020/556-3000. $$.*

Canal Bike Rentals & Rules

Canal bikes seat up to five people. They are stable and comfortable. The charge is 8€ per person per hour for one or two people, and 7€ per person per hour for three or four people. The above itinerary will take about 2 hours, a bit longer if you go slowly. You'll need a credit card, a 50€ refundable deposit (which can go on the card), and an ID to rent your canal bike. Rental hours are 10am to 9:30pm June to September and 10am to 6pm the rest of the year (in winter only when the weather is tolerable). Rent from Canal Bike, at the Rijksmuseum Mooring (☎ 020/626-5574; www.canal.nl). In addition to this mooring, there are docks in front of the Anne Frank House, Leidseplein (facing the American Hotel), and at the corner of Keizersgracht and Leidsestraat. If you get tired, you can always drop off your canal bike at one of these moorings and receive your refundable deposit back.

Always stay to the right in the canals—this is especially important when going under bridges in narrow canals. All other traffic has a right of way. The port area is off-limits to canal bikes. If you need a break, stop at one of the mooring docks. **Never** leave your canal bike unattended—it will be towed away.

Biking Along the **Amstel River**

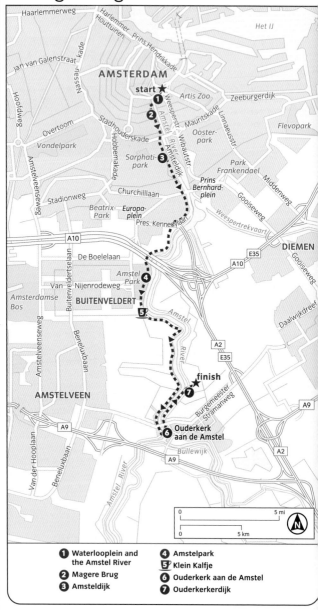

1 Waterlooplein and the Amstel River
2 Magere Brug
3 Amsteldijk
4 Amstelpark
5 Klein Kalfje
6 Ouderkerk aan de Amstel
7 Ouderkerkerdijk

A msterdammers go everywhere on their bikes and don't particularly enjoy it when inexperienced visitors on a rented *fiets* (as a bicycle is called here) attempt to navigate the inner city's complicated streets and alleyways. This bike route takes you away from the city center and out to more pleasant and tranquil surroundings. START: **Tram no. 9 or 14 to Waterlooplein.**

1 Waterlooplein and the Amstel River. Once you've rented your bikes (see the box "Renting Your Bikes," below), head south along the Amstel on Amsteldijk. Keep your eye out for houseboats moored along both banks and for a lot of other boat activity on the river. The Amstel will be to your left; on the return, you'll be on the far bank, with the river on your right.

2 ★ Magere Brug (Skinny Bridge). The Skinny Bridge over the Amstel is actually an 18th-century replacement of the original 17th-century bridge. It's a double drawbridge made of African azobe wood. Hundreds of lights illuminate the bridge at night. The Theater Carré, one of the city's largest theaters, is visible from the bridge.

Enjoy peaceful views of canals and the river as you pedal through the city.

Traveling the city by bike is a way of life for many Amsterdammers.

3 Amsteldijk. As you pedal south, you'll need to cross busy Stadhouderskade. Continue on Amsteldijk south to the Berlagebrug (Berlage Bridge), where the traffic thickens again. Stay on Amsteldijk—most of the road traffic swings away to the right on President Kennedy-laan. The road becomes noticeably quieter, almost rural, and you can relax and admire the many houseboats lined along the banks of the river.

4 Amstelpark. Go under the highway bridge (A10 ring road) and continue along the riverbank until you reach this often quiet park. There's a statue of Rembrandt and a windmill at the end of the park, so continue pedaling to the south until you see them. It's a classic Dutch scene and perfect for a little rest and a photo or two.

5 Klein Kalfje. At this point you'll probably want to stretch out your legs and have a snack. This little Dutch cafe-restaurant has a great riverside terrace mere steps from the canal barges moored alongside it. Try the Dutch pea soup or spicy sausages with hot mustard. Consider fueling up for your ride back with a strong Dutch coffee. *Amsteldijk 355.* ☎ *020/644-5338. $.*

6 ★ Ouderkerk aan de Amstel. Continue south, past villas and cottages, to this charming little village. If you have time, lock up your bikes by the river and meander through the village streets before heading back.

7 Ouderkerkerdijk. Head back north on the opposite bank. You'll find this a quieter and narrower road than the Amsteldijk, with much less traffic. When you reach the Berlagebrug again, you'll know you're getting close to your starting point. The streets are busier here,

You can usually bike for a whole day for under 10€ if you get your bike back to the rental shop before closing time.

but stay on the right bank and enjoy the different vistas until you reach Waterlooplein. ●

Renting Your Bikes

The rental outlet closest to your starting point is MacBike at Mr. Visserplein 2 (☎ 020/620-0985; www.macbike.nl). To get there, take tram no. 9 or 14 to Waterlooplein. You'll need a passport and a 50€ deposit (cash or credit card; the deposit is refundable upon return of the bike). Rates begin at 7€ for 3 hours and 9.50€ for 1 day. **MacBike** is open daily 9am to 5:45pm. The 1-day rental requires you to return the bike by closing time. A range of bikes is available, including tandems and six-speed touring bikes. There's another MacBike at Stationsplein 12 outside Centraal Station (☎ 020/620-0985).

Dining **Best Bets**

Best **Herring Sandwich**
Eetsalon Van Dobben $ *Korte Reguliersdwarsstraat 5–9 (p 96)*

Best **Canal View**
De Belhamel $$ *Brouwersgracht 60 (p 95)*

Best **When Money Is No Object**
★★★ La Rive $$$$ *Professor Tulpplein 1 (p 98)*

Best **Dutch Oysters from Zeeland**
★ Le Pêcheur $$$ *Reguliersdwarsstraat 32 (p 98)*

Best **Place for Dining with Your Shoes Off**
★ Supper Club $$ *Jonge Roelensteeg 21 (p 99)*

Best **Young Celebrity Chef Hot Spot**
★★ Fifteen Amsterdam $$$ *Pakhuis Amsterdam, Jollemanhof 9 (p 97)*

Best **Innovative Five-Course Menu**
★★ Bordewijk $$$$ *Noordermarkt 7 (p 94)*

Best **Drop-Dead Gorgeous Decor**
★★ Vinkeles $$$$ *Keizersgracht 384 (p 96)*

Best **Upmarket Moroccan Cuisine**
★ Mamouche $$ *Quellijnstraat 104 (p 98)*

Best for **Trendy Parents with No Babysitter**
★ Bloesem $$ *Binnen Dommersstraat 13 (p 94)*

Best **Traditional Dutch Pea Soup**
Brasserie De Poort $$ *Nieuwezijds Voorburgwal 176–180 (p 95)*

Best **Vegetarian**
Golden Temple $ *Utrechtsestraat 126 (p 97)*

Best **Fancy Breakfast or Fabulous English Tea**
★ Pulitzers $$$ *Keizersgracht 234 (p 99)*

Best **Fashionistas**
★ Caffe PC $$ *Pieter Cornelisz Hooftstraat 87 (p 95)*

Best for **Dining Alfresco**
★★ De Kas $$$ *Kamerlingh Onneslaan 3 (p 96)*

Best for **Kids**
Pancake Bakery $ *Prinsengracht 191 (p 99)*

Best **Late-Night Chinese**
Nam Kee $ *Zeedijk 111–113 (p 98)*

Best **Elegant Indonesian**
★ Sama Sebo $$ *Pieter Cornelisz Hooftstraat 27 (p 99)*

Previous page: The dining room at the Grand Hotel.
This page: Try a herring sandwich the way the locals eat them—with onion and pickles.

Museum District **Dining**

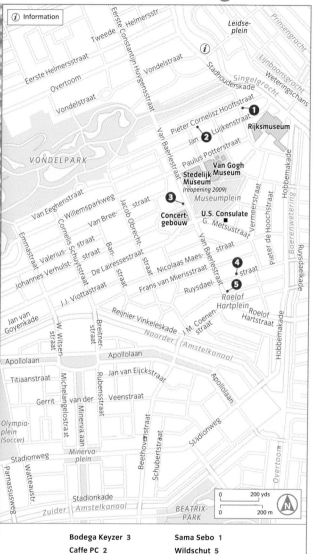

Bodega Keyzer 3   Sama Sebo 1

Caffe PC 2   Wildschut 5

Le Garage 4

Central Amsterdam **Dining**

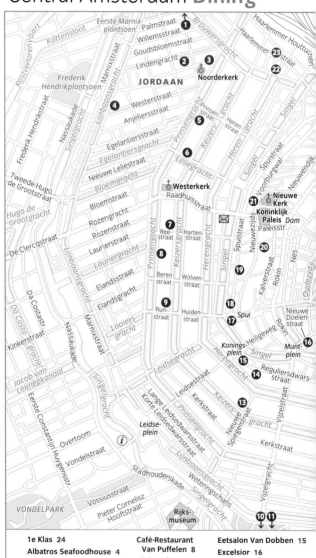

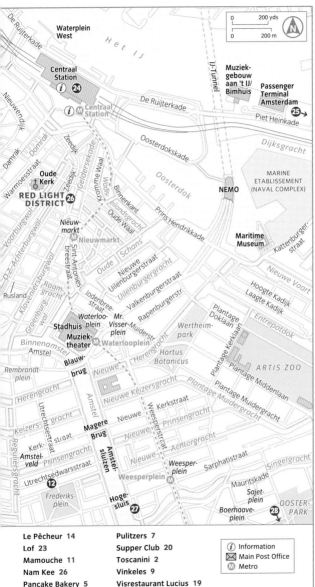

Le Pêcheur 14
Lof 23
Mamouche 11
Nam Kee 26
Pancake Bakery 5
Pasta e Basta 13

Pulitzers 7
Supper Club 20
Toscanini 2
Vinkeles 9
Visrestaurant Lucius 19

ⓘ Information
✉ Main Post Office
Ⓜ Metro

Amsterdam Restaurants A to Z

★ **Albatros Seafoodhouse** JOR-DAAN *SEAFOOD* The Atlantic and North Sea fish served here have the great virtue of being grilled, poached, and fried in the simplest manner possible, and then served in ship-ahoy decor (or on a sidewalk terrace) by friendly old-timers in a relaxed neighborhood atmosphere. Try the mixed seafood salad, the raw herring, or the sea bass. Reservations recommended. *Westerstraat 264 (at Lijnbaansgracht).* ☎ *020/627-9932. www.restaurantalbatros. nl. Entrees 16€–23€ (some prices set daily). AE, DC, MC, V. Dinner Thurs–Mon. Tram: 3 or 10 to Marnixplein. Map p 92.*

★ kids **Bloesem** OLD CENTER *FUSION* Hip and elegant, Bloesem serves up an unusual brand of cuisine: European fusion, with offerings such as garlic soup with chorizo, duck confit with sauerkraut, or a Belgian endive salad with Valencia oranges. This is one of the few trendy Amsterdam eateries that embraces kids. *Binnen Dommersstraat 13.* ☎ *020/770-0407. www. restaurantbloesem.nl. Entrees 16€–20€; fixed-price menus 33€–37€. AE, MC, V. Dinner Wed–Sun. Tram: 3 to Haarlemmerstraat. Map p 92.*

Bodega Keyzer MUSEUM DISTRICT *DUTCH/INTERNATIONAL* A classic choice near the Concertgebouw, this 100-year-old restaurant with dark, dusky decor and starched pink linens serves fresh fish, hare, and venison along with the usual international favorites. *Van Baerlestraat 96 (beside the Concertgebouw).* ☎ *020/671-1441. Entrees 20€–33€; fixed-price menu 33€. AE, DC, MC, V. Breakfast, lunch & dinner Mon–Sat; lunch & dinner Sun. Tram: 3, 5, 12, 16, or 24 to Museumplein. Map p 91.*

★★ **Bordewijk** JORDAAN *FRENCH FUSION* This trendy restaurant pulls in affluent locals who come here for the creative cuisine, fine cheeses, and superb wine list. If you're a laid-back gourmand, you've found your nirvana, especially in summer, when you can dine alfresco. Specialties include a bouillabaisse Marseillaise with a variety of shellfish and a salted rib roast with bordelaise sauce. There are usually a few Asian-influenced dishes and a sushi-style appetizer. Reservations required. *Noordermarkt 7 (at Prinsengracht).* ☎ *020/624-3899. www.bordewijk.nl. Entrees 20€–30€; fixed-price menus 39€–54€. AE, MC, V. Dinner Tues–Sun. Tram: 1,*

Be sure to sample a variety of Dutch cheeses while you're in Amsterdam.

2, 5, 13, or 17 to Martelaarsgracht. Map p 92.

Brasserie De Poort OLD CENTER *DUTCH* For over a 100 years, this former beer hall has served straightforward Dutch cuisine in a traditional setting complete with Delft blue tiles. Pea soup, lamb, and steaks are the highlights. *In the Hotel Die Port van Cleve, Nieuwezijds Voorburgwal 176–180.* ☎ *020/622-6429. www.dieportvancleve. com. Entrees 14€–28€; fixed-price menus 29€–36€. AE, DC, MC, V. Breakfast, lunch & dinner daily. Tram: 1, 2, 5, 13, 14, or 17 to the Dam. Map p 92.*

★ **Café Luxembourg** OLD CENTER *DUTCH/INTERNATIONAL* At one of the most glamorous grand cafes in the city, you'll find a very reasonably priced selection of well-prepared straightforward dishes such as meatloaf, Indonesian grilled chicken, omelets, salads, and sandwiches. Great for breakfast and lingering over cups of strong coffee with a newspaper. *Spuistraat 24 (at Spui).* ☎ *020/620-6264. www.cafe luxembourg.nl. Entrees 8€–15€. AE, DC, MC, V. Breakfast, lunch & dinner daily. Tram: 1, 2, or 5 to Spui. Map p 92.*

Café-Restaurant Van Puffelen CANAL BELT *DUTCH/INTERNA-TIONAL* This brown cafe serves delicious dishes with a creative flair, such as fried butterfish with a tarragon-and-coriander sauce or the house salad with tandoori chicken and Cajun shrimp. Food served until midnight. *Prinsengracht 377.* ☎ *020/624-6270. www.goodfoodgroup.nl. Entrees 13€–21€; fixed-price menu 21€. Dinner Mon–Fri; lunch & dinner Sat–Sun. Tram: 13, 14, or 17 to West-ermarkt. Map p 92.*

★ **Caffe PC** MUSEUM DISTRICT/ VONDELPARK *INTERNATIONAL* Smack dab in the middle of

In summer, you'll find plenty of opportunities to dine alfresco.

Amsterdam's most elegant shopping street, you can take your place among the absolutely fabulous models and fashion gurus and sip on a martini while indulging in tapas and fresh salads. *Pieter Cornelisz Hooftstraat 87.* ☎ *020/673-4752. www.caffepc.nl. Entrees 11€–23€. AE, MC, V. Breakfast, lunch & dinner Tues–Sat; breakfast & lunch Sun; lunch Mon. Tram: 2 or 5 to Hobbe-mastraat. Map p 91.*

★★ **Christophe** CANAL BELT *FRENCH/MEDITERRANEAN* Ultra-refined but with a modern flair best describes the cuisine at French chef Jean-Joel Bonsens's elegant restaurant. North African *tajine* and Italian parmesan cheese have a place on the menu, alongside French "staples" like Vendée roast duck. Reservations required. *Lelliegracht 46 (btw. Prinsengracht & Keizersgracht).* ☎ *020/625-0807. www.restaurant christophe.nl. Entrees 29€–36€. AE, DC, MC, V. Dinner Tues–Sat. Tram: 13, 14, or 17 to Westermarkt. Map p 92.*

★ **De Belhamel** CANAL BELT *INTERNATIONAL* If you score a window table, you'll have a terribly romantic view of the junction of two canals. The eclectic menu changes often and includes both meat and

Vinkeles restaurant.

vegetarian dishes. Appetizers may include puffed pastries layered with smoked salmon, roasted crayfish tails, and steamed mussels. For a main course, the beef tenderloin in Madeira sauce with zucchini rosti and roasted garlic is a specialty. *Brouwersgracht 60 (at Herengracht).* ☎ *020/622-1095. www.belhamel.nl. Entrees 22€–25€; fixed-price menus 35€–45€. AE, MC, V. Dinner daily. Tram: 1, 2, 5, 13, or 17 to Martelaarsgracht. Map p 92.*

★ **De Duvel** PIJP *FUSION* Packed with hip and trendy locals, De Duvel (the Devil) serves excellent food in a cozy red dining room. Peanut-pumpkin soup and mushrooms filled with snails are some of the more daring dishes. You'll also find a daily selection of pasta, seafood, and chicken offerings. *Eerste Van der Helststraat 59–61.* ☎ *020/675-7517. www.de duvel.nl. Entrees 15€–19€. AE, DC, MC, V. Lunch Tues–Sun; dinner daily. Tram: 16 or 24 to Albert Cuypstraat. Map p 92.*

★★ **De Kas** AMSTERDAM SOUTH *INTERNATIONAL* In summer the huge outdoor patio seats over 100 guests adjacent to the fragrant herb gardens. The interior is light and airy (it was formerly a greenhouse) and the menu changes daily. Appetizers may include an eggplant terrine with chèvre and red-pepper

coulis; main courses may include a roasted monkfish with a ratatouille of fresh vegetables from the garden or a leg of lamb with polenta and spinach. If it's in season, try the heavenly rhubarb soup for dessert. Reservations recommended. *Kamerlingh Onneslaan 3 (close to Amstel Station).* ☎ *020/462-4562. www. restaurantdekas.nl. Fixed-price lunch 35€; fixed-price dinner 48€. AE, DC, MC, V. Lunch Mon–Fri; dinner Mon–Sat. Tram: 9 to Hogeweg. Map p 92.*

★★ **Vinkeles** CANAL BELT *FRENCH* This place is ultrachic and ultrahip, not to mention ultraexpensive. Top chef Dennis Kuipers whips up dishes such as roasted Anjou pigeon with spices and dried apricots. Reservations required. *In the Dylan Hotel, Keizersgracht 384.* ☎ *020/530-2010. www.vinkeles.com. Entrees 26€–44€. AE, DC, MC, V. Lunch Mon–Fri; dinner Mon–Sat. Tram: 1, 2, or 5 to Spui. Map p 93.*

Eetsalon Van Dobben OLD CENTER *DUTCH FAST FOOD* This is more of a sandwich place than a restaurant, but some patrons swear by the platter of giant meatballs. Locals come here for herring, liverwurst, croquets, or ox-tongue sandwiches. Simpler roast beef and Gouda sandwiches are also available. *Korte Reguliersdwarsstraat*

5–9. ☎ 020/624-4200. *Entrees 6€–8€; sandwiches 2.50€–4.50€. No credit cards. Lunch & dinner daily. Tram: 4, 9, or 14 to Rembrandtplein. Map p 92.*

★★★ **Excelsior** OLD CENTER *FRENCH* Amsterdam's most formal restaurant requires a jacket for men and deep pockets for whoever foots the bill. Crystal chandeliers, crisp linens, and picture windows overlooking the river make for a romantic setting. Expect to dine on such delicacies as foie gras, smoked eel, sweetbreads of lamb, halibut, and veal, all prepared to perfection. Reservations recommended. *In the Hotel de l'Europe, Nieuwe Doelenstraat 2–8 (facing Muntplein).* ☎ *020/531-1777. www.restaurantexcelsior. nl. Entrees 34€–42€; fixed-price menus 49€–95€. AE, DC, MC, V. Breakfast, lunch & dinner Mon–Fri; breakfast & dinner Sat–Sun. Tram: 4, 9, 14, 16, 24, or 25 to Muntplein. Map p 92.*

★★ **Fifteen Amsterdam** WATERFRONT *INTERNATIONAL* London celebrity chef Jamie Oliver's hot spot has both a full-menu restaurant and an adjoining trattoria serving less elaborate (and less expensive) fare. Drop-dead gorgeous staff, clientele, and food, with dishes like a salad of the day with figs, prosciutto,

Gorgonzola, and toasted almonds on field greens; seafood risotto; linguini with horse mushrooms and thyme; and pan-fried calves' liver with balsamic figs and pancetta. Reservations are required for the restaurant. *Pakhuis Amsterdam, Jollemanhof 9.* ☎ *0900/343-8336. www.fifteen.nl. Restaurant fixed-price menu 46€; trattoria entrees 23€–29€. AE, DC, MC, V. Restaurant dinner daily (closed Sun mid-July to mid-Aug); trattoria dinner Sun–Thurs. Tram: 10 or 26 to Rietlandpark. Map p 92.*

Golden Temple CANAL BELT *VEGETARIAN* Into its fourth decade, this is still one of the best vegetarian (and vegan) options in town. If anything, the atmosphere is a tad too hallowed, an effect enhanced by a minimalist approach to decorative flourishes. The menu livens things up, with its unlikely roster of Indian, Middle Eastern, and Mexican dishes. Multiple-choice platters are a good way to go. *Utrechtsestraat 126 (2 blocks south of Prinsengracht).* ☎ *020/626-8560. Entrees 10€–15€; mixed platter 15€. MC, V. Dinner daily. Tram: 4 to Prinsengracht. Map p 92.*

★ **Kantjil & de Tijger** OLD CENTER *INDONESIAN* Unlike Holland's many Indonesian restaurants that wear their ethnic origins on their sleeves, with staffers decked out in

Celebrity chef Jamie Oliver's Fifteen Amsterdam restaurant.

traditional costume, the Antelope and the Tiger is chic and modern. A bestseller in this popular eatery is the 20-item *rijsttafel* for two. Reservations recommended for Friday and Saturday evening. *Spuistraat 291–293 (at Spui).* ☎ *020/620-0994. www.kantjil.nl. Entrees 13€–16€; rijsttafels 43€–55€ for 2. AE, DC, MC, V. Dinner Mon–Fri; lunch & dinner Sat–Sun. Tram: 1, 2, or 5 to Spui. Map p 92.*

★★★ **La Rive** OOST *FRENCH/ MEDITERRANEAN* Service at the city's top-rated restaurant can be as stiff as the ironed linens. Nevertheless, you'll dine like royalty on specials like grilled baby abalone with citrus-pickled onion purée or grill-roasted rack of lamb with dates. Reservations required. *In the Amstel InterContinental Hotel, Professor Tulpplein 1 (off Weesperstraat).* ☎ *020/ 520-3264. www.restaurantlarive.nl. Entrees 47€–73€; fixed-price menus 85€–113€. AE, DC, MC, V. Lunch Mon–Fri; dinner Mon–Sat. Tram: 7 or 10 to Sarphatistraat. Map p 92.*

★★ **Le Garage** MUSEUM DISTRICT *FUSION* The hottest restaurant in town serves up creative fusion dishes (such as tuna tartare with curry or a crisp spinach pancake) in a setting with bright lights and big mirrors that's reminiscent of Las Vegas or Tokyo. Call way ahead for dinner reservations (which are required) or come for lunch when it's quieter. *Ruysdaelstraat 54–56 (at Van Baerlestraat).* ☎ *020/679-7176. www.restaurantlegarage.nl. Entrees 25€–47€; fixed-price menu 45€. AE, DC, MC, V. Lunch Mon–Fri; dinner daily. Tram: 3, 5, 12, or 24 to Roelof Hartplein. Map p 91.*

★ **Le Pêcheur** OLD CENTER *SEAFOOD* The focus in this airy, tranquil restaurant is less on presentation and more on freshness and taste. Come here for house-smoked salmon, or fresh oysters and mussels from the Dutch province of Zeeland. Extensive wine list. *Reguliersdwarsstraat 32 (behind the Flower Market).* ☎ *020/624-3121. www.lepecheur.nl. Entrees 22€–40€. AE, MC, V. Lunch Mon–Fri; dinner Mon–Sat. Tram: 1, 2, or 5 to Koningsplein. Map p 92.*

★ **Lof** OLD CENTER *FUSION* The menu changes daily depending on what's fresh at local markets. The delicious offerings include one vegetarian specialty. If you're lucky, you'll find the appetizer of white asparagus topped with a poached egg on the menu. For a main course, the roasted cod with black olive and anchovies with capers and pecorino is both delicate and satisfying; the shaved slices of leg of lamb on fresh morels is outstanding. Try one of the luscious homemade tortes for dessert. *Haarlemmerstraat 62.* ☎ *020/620-2997. Entrees 12€–22€; fixed-price menu 35€. No credit cards. Dinner Tues–Sun. Tram: 1, 2, 5, 6, 13, or 17 to Martelaarsgracht. Map p 92.*

★ **Mamouche** PIJP *MOROCCAN* You'll find exceptionally good Moroccan cuisine in this elegant neighborhood restaurant. Try the lamb tagine with prunes, almonds, olives, and lentils; the rabbit with apricot and cinnamon; or the vegetable couscous. *Quellijnstraat 104.* ☎ *020/673-6361. www.restaurant mamouche.nl. Entrees 17€–23€. AE, MC, V. Dinner daily. Tram: 16 or 24 to Stadhouderskade. Map p 92.*

Nam Kee OLD CENTER *CHINESE* Don't let the drab, neon-lit dining room dissuade you from trying the very good, fresh food here. Service is fast and they're open late, so you can dine until midnight. I love the duck with plum sauce. *Zeedijk 111–113.* ☎ *020/624-3470. www. namkee.nl. Entrees 6€–16€. AE, MC, V. Lunch & dinner daily. Metro: Nieuwmarkt. Map p 92.*

1e Klas (Eerste Klas) OLD CENTER *INTERNATIONAL* This Art Nouveau restaurant was a waiting room for first-class rail passengers in the late 1800s. Now it's a great place for a drink, a snack, or a full meal, and it's just steps from the trains. The club sandwich and the Caesar salad here are delicious but if you're after a hot meal, the beef stroganoff or the Dover sole with fries are good choices. *Platform 2B, inside Centraal Station.* ☎ *020/625-0131. Entrees 8€–15€. No credit cards. Breakfast, lunch & dinner daily. Tram: 1, 2, 4, 5, 9, 13, 16, 17, 24, 25, or 26 to Centraal Station. Map p 92.*

kids Pancake Bakery CANAL BELT *PANCAKES* A 17th-century canal warehouse is home to this simple bakery where you can sample yummy pancakes with all kinds of toppings, from curried turkey with pineapple to honey, nuts, and whipped cream. *Prinsengracht 191.* ☎ *020/625-1333. www.pancake.nl. Pancakes 5€–12€. AE, MC, V. Lunch & dinner daily. Tram: 13, 14, or 17 to Westermarkt. Map p 92.*

★ Pasta e Basta CANAL BELT *ITALIAN* This cozy, candlelit Italian restaurant has the best opera-singing waiters this side of La Scala. The fantastic antipasti buffet is served out of an antique grand piano and the main courses include a delicious Gorgonzola lasagna with Parma ham and fresh basil. *Nieuwe Spiegelstraat 8.* ☎ *020/422-2222. www.pastaebasta.com. Entrees 13€–27€; fixed-price menus 50€–55€. AE, MC, V. Dinner daily. Tram: 16, 24, or 25 to Keizersgracht. Map p 92.*

★ Pulitzers CANAL BELT *GOURMET* You'll find this trendy restaurant inside the drop-dead gorgeous Hotel Pulitzer. I recommend coming for the full buffet breakfast, served until 2pm, or afternoon tea complete with

Pasta e Basta's generous antipasti buffet.

crumpets, clotted cream, and cucumber sandwiches. An innovative lunch and dinner menu is also available. Reservations recommended. *Keizersgracht 234.* ☎ *020/523-5235. www.starwoodhotels.com. Entrees 12€–25€. AE, DC, MC, V. Breakfast, lunch & dinner daily. Tram: 13, 14, or 17 to Westermarkt. Map p 92.*

★ Sama Sebo MUSEUM DISTRICT/ VONDELPARK *INDONESIAN* This upmarket Indonesian restaurant is decorated with rush mats and batiks and serves an unrivaled 23-plate rijsttafel (a feast consisting of rice and many accompanying dishes like curried meats, fish, vegetables, and nuts) just a few steps from the Rijksmuseum. *Pieter Cornelisz Hooftstraat 27.* ☎ *020/662-8146. www. samasebo.nl. Entrees 14€–21€; rijsttafel 28€. AE, DC, MC, V. Lunch & dinner Mon–Sat. Tram: 2 or 5 to Hobbemastraat. Map p 91.*

★ Supper Club OLD CENTER *FUSION* Kick back in this ultramodern, blindingly white, hypertrendy restaurant, stretch out on couches and cushions, and groove along to whatever the DJ is spinning. There's no telling what the chefs (called "food magicians") will whip up—you inform your waiter of any dietary

The dining room at the Pulitzer.

restrictions and wait to see what arrives on your table (typical dishes include pea soup or Parma ham with melon for an appetizer, and seared tuna on greens or chicken with a sweet and sour sauce with roasted vegetables for a main course). The atmosphere and not the food is the highlight here. Reservations recommended. *Jonge Roelensteeg 21.* ☎ *020/344-6400. www.supperclub.nl. Fixed-price menus 65€–70€. AE, DC, MC, V. Dinner daily. Tram: 1, 2, 5, 13, 14, or 17 to the Dam. Map p 92.*

★**Toscanini** JORDAAN *ITALIAN* This small, charming eatery has an open kitchen and a warm and welcoming ambience. Authentic Italian dishes include veal lasagna, seafood risotto, a selection of fresh fish, and many excellent pastas. *Lindengracht 75 (off Brouwersgracht).* ☎ *020/623-2813. www.toscanini.nu. Entrees 16€–20€; fixed-price menu 43€. AE, DC, MC, V. Dinner Mon–Sat. Tram: 1, 2, 5, 13, or 17 to Martelaarsgracht. Map p 92.*

Visrestaurant Lucius OLD CENTER *SEAFOOD* A solid choice for fresh seafood, Lucius offers oysters and lobsters imported from Norway and Canada. The spectacular seafood platter includes mussels, oysters, clams, shrimp, and a half lobster. *Spuistraat 247 (near Spui).* ☎ *020/624-1831. www.lucius.nl. Entrees 19€–27€; fixed-price menu 38€. AE, DC, MC, V. Dinner daily. Tram: 1, 2, or 5 to Spui. Map p 92.*

Wildschut MUSEUM DISTRICT *INTERNATIONAL* Wildschut is great any time of day but especially on summer evenings when the large terrace is open. You'll find vegetarian lasagna, large salads, and good sandwiches here, but the people-watching is more interesting than the food. *Roelof Hartplein 1–3 (off Van Baerlestraat).* ☎ *020/676-8220. Entrees 8€–24€. MC, V. Breakfast, lunch & dinner Mon–Fri; lunch & dinner Sat–Sun. Tram: 3, 5, 12, or 24 to Roelof Hartplein. Map p 91.* ●

Some of the 20-odd dishes you might find at an Indonesian rijsttafel.

7 The Best Nightlife

Nightlife Best Bets

Best Place to Sip Martinis with the Young & the Beautiful
★★ Arc, *Reguliersdwarsstraat 44* (p 106)

Best Place to Drink with the Locals
★ Café Nol, *Westerstraat 109 (p 106)*

Friendliest Gay Bar
★ Amstel FiftyFour, *Amstel 54* (p 109)

Best Irish Pub
O'Donnell's Irish Pub, *Ferdinand Bolstraat 5 (p 110)*

Dance Club That's Most Worth a Taxi Ride
★★ Tonight, *'s-Gravesandestraat 51* (p 109)

Best Brown Cafe with a Summer Terrace
★ Café De Twee Prinsen, *Prinsenstraat 27 (p 107)*

Best Place to Dance if You're Looking for Exclusivity
The Mansion, *Hobbemastraat 2* (p 108)

Most Hip & Happening Dance Club
★★ Panama, *Oostelijke Handelskade 4 (p 108)*

Best for Romance
★ Chocolate Bar, *Eerste Van der Helststraat 62A (p 106)*

Best for Expats
Three Sisters Grand Pub, *Leidseplein 2 (p 110)*

Best Lesbian Bar
★ Vive-la-Vie, *Amstelstraat 7* (p 109)

Best House-Brewed Beer
★ In de Wildeman, *Kolksteeg 3* (p 108)

Best Place for a Drink after Midnight
★★ Panama, *Oostelijke Handelskade 4 (p 108)*

Best Happy Hour
Hoppe, *Spui 18–20 (p 107)*

Previous page: Drinking at one of Amsterdam's sophisticated nightspots.
This page: See the "Cannabis Tolerance" box on p 110 for information on Amsterdam's "coffee shops," another popular nighttime option.

Pijp Nightlife

Chocolate Bar **3**

Helden **2**

O'Donnell's Irish Pub **1**

| 0 | 200 yds |
| 0 | 200 m |

Central Amsterdam Nightlife

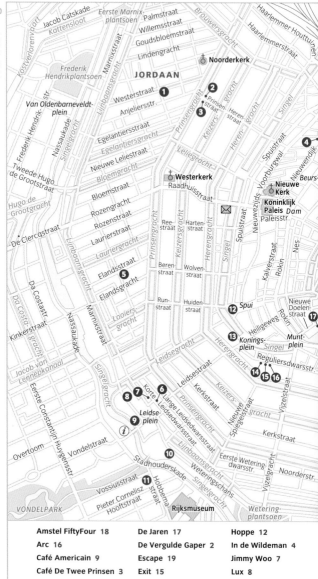

Amstel FiftyFour 18	De Jaren 17	Hoppe 12
Arc 16	De Vergulde Gaper 2	In de Wildeman 4
Café Americain 9	Escape 19	Jimmy Woo 7
Café De Twee Prinsen 3	Exit 15	Lux 8
Café Nol 1	Home 21	The Mansion 11

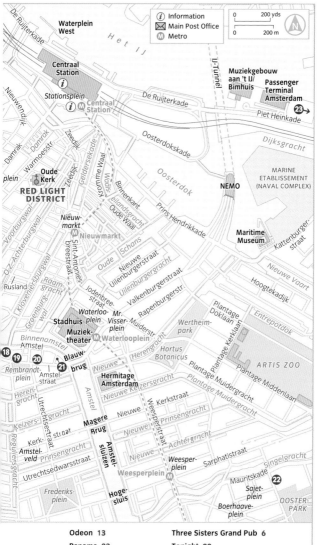

Nightlife A to Z

Bars

★★ Arc OLD CENTER One of the most attractive and trendy bars in the city pulls in some gay clients as well. The friendly, 20- and 30-something mixed crowd is very hip. Many opt to lounge the night away here and indulge in the delicious appetizer platters. *Reguliersdwarsstraat 44.* ☎ *020/689-7070. www.bararc.com. Tram: 1, 2, or 5 to Koningsplein. Map p 104.*

★★ Café Americain LEIDSEPLEIN This Amsterdam institution is a grand place for drinks in the evenings, though be warned that it's frequented heavily by tourists. *Amsterdam American Hotel, Leidsekade 97.* ☎ *020/556-3000. www.amsterdam american.com. Tram: 1, 2, 5, 7, or 10 to Leidseplein. Map p 104.*

Café Nol JORDAAN This cafe is more like a relaxed bar. It caters to a mix of young, cool Jordaaners and old-timers who have lived in the neighborhood for ages. The kitsch interior includes crystal chandeliers, mirrors, a red carpet, and hanging potted plants. Great place to observe young yuppies in action. *Westerstraat 109.* ☎ *020/624-5380. Tram: 3 or 10 to Marnixplein. Map p 104.*

★ Chocolate Bar PIJP The hippest bar in the Pijp also serves up delicious light meals. DJs spin great music Thursday through Saturday, and there's a terrace for when the weather's fine. *Eerste Van der Helststraat 62A.* ☎ *020/675-7672. www.chocolate-bar.nl. Tram: 16 or 24 to Albert Cuypstraat. Map p 103.*

★★ De Jaren OLD CENTER On the Binnenamstel waterfront, this postmodern spot is big and sunny, with a panoramic upper-floor terrace where the young and hip lounge in sweet anonymity. There's a great salad bar, soups, and good daily quiches, and a separate restaurant. *Nieuwe Doelenstraat 20–22 (at Muntplein).* ☎ *020/625-5771. www. cafe-de-jaren.nl. Tram: 4, 9, 14, 16, 24, or 25 to Muntplein. Map p 104.*

★ Lux LEIDSEPLEIN Although the Leidseplein area is quite touristy,

The average price for a beer in Amsterdam is 1.50€ to 3€ (hip clubs and hotel bars will likely charge more).

Brown cafes get their name from their smoke-stained walls.

laid-back Lux draws in a healthy dose of locals with its chic attitude. Sit on the upper level to enjoy a sweeping view of the place. *Marnixstraat 403.* ☎ *020/422-1412. Tram: 1, 2, 5, 7, or 10 to Leidseplein. Map p 104.*

★ **Helden** PIJP   A young well-heeled crowd sinks into the sofas and sips martinis and mojitos over soft music at this trendy place. The food's good, too, and there's a pleasant summer terrace where you can lounge alfresco. *Eerste Van der Helstraat 42.* ☎ *020/673-3332. www.helden.nu. Tram: 16 or 24 to Stadhouderskade. Map p 103.*

Brown Cafes

★ **Café De Twee Prinsen** CANAL BELT   This attractive brown cafe has mosaic-tiled floors and a wood-muraled ceiling. I like to while away a warm evening on the enchanting summer terrace overlooking Prinsengracht. There's usually a healthy mix of local intellectuals and visitors, from young backpackers to middle-aged professionals. *Prinsenstraat 27.* ☎ *020/624-9722. Tram: 1, 2, 5, 13, or 17 to Martelaarsgracht. Map p 104.*

De Vergulde Gaper CANAL BELT   On warm nights the terrace right beside the Prinsengracht is the place to be for 30- and 40-something professionals, and the interior is cozy, too, decorated with vintage

posters and old medicine bottles (it used to be a pharmacy). *Prinsenstraat 30.* ☎ *020/624-8975. Tram: 1, 2, 5, 13, or 17 to Martelaarsgracht. Map p 104.*

Hoppe OLD CENTER   This historic brown cafe, dating back to 1670, has a convivial, smoky atmosphere. It's often crowded, especially with the after-work crowd, so expect standing room only in the early evenings. It gets boisterous here when the professionals leave; most of the patrons who end up staying late are young students traveling around Europe. *Spui 18–20.* ☎ *020/420-4420. Tram: 1, 2, or 5 to Spui. Map p 104.*

A friendly neighborhood brown cafe can be a great place to mix with locals.

Pick up a copy of Amsterdam Day by Day *at the tourist office for the scoop on Amsterdam's hottest clubs.*

★ **In de Wildeman** OLD CENTER
This historic brown cafe originated in 1690 and has its original tile floor and rows of bottles from when it functioned as a distillery. It boasts 17 draft and 200 bottled beers from around the world. It's a laid-back atmosphere, with mostly hard-drinking but very friendly locals ranging from 30- to 50-something. *Kolksteeg 3.* ☎ *020/638-2348. www.inde wildeman.nl. Tram: 1, 2, 5, 13, or 17 to Nieuwezijds Kolk. Map p 104.*

Dance Clubs

★★ **Escape** REMBRANDTPLEIN
Three dance floors, a great sound system, and a healthy mix of local and international DJs make this one of the prime choices for the young and trendy. Saturday is especially popular. *Rembrandtplein 11.* ☎ *020/ 622-1111. www.escape.nl. Cover 8€–20€. Tram: 4, 9, or 14 to Rembrandtplein. Map p 104.*

Home REMBRANDTPLEIN This ultratrendy place tends to attract Dutch celebs (and wannabes) and offers a variety of music on its three floors, depending on the night—but the main deal here is house. *Wagenstraat 3–7.* ☎ *020/620-1375.*

www.clubhome.nl. Cover 10€–12€. Tram: 4, 9, or 14 to Rembrandtplein. Map p 104.

★ **Jimmy Woo** LEIDSEPLEIN This antique-looking, Hong Kong–style club attracts a slow-burning crowd, but the slow-starting music gets spikier and the vibes begin to smolder the later it gets. Guest-list entry only some nights makes this deluxe spot occasionally hard to get into. *Korte Leidsedwarsstraat 18.* ☎ *020/ 626-3150. www.jimmywoo.com. Cover 15€–20€. Tram: 1, 2, 5, 7, or 10 to Leidseplein. Map p 104.*

★ **Odeon** CANAL BELT Inside this converted 17th-century canal house, you'll find period ceiling paintings and stucco decor. You'll also find three dance floors, each offering a different kind of music: classic disco, jazz, and house. *Singel 460.* ☎ *020/ 521-8555. www.odeontheater.nl. Cover 6€–12€. Tram: 1, 2, or 5 to Koningsplein. Map p 104.*

★★ **Panama** WATERFRONT A historic 1899 building that used to be a power station houses this hip club. The attractive bar/restaurant in the lobby opens up into the cavernous club, which hosts big-name DJs and special events, depending on the day and seasons. This is a see-and-be seen place for 30- to 40-something professionals. So dress to impress and bring some attitude. Call ahead for program information. *Oostelijke Handelskade 4.* ☎ *020/ 311-8686. www.panama.nl. Cover 10€–25€. Tram: 10 or 26 to Rietlandpark. Map p 104.*

★ **The Mansion** LEIDSEPLEIN
Hotshot DJs jet in from around Europe for this swank venue's Friday and Saturday club nights. At other times, the former royal mansion on the edge of Vondelpark, which dates from 1905, gets by on its suite of überplush restaurants and cocktail bars. *Hobbemastraat 2.* ☎ *020/616-6664.*

www.the-mansion.nl. Cover 15€–25€. Tram: 2 or 5 to Hobbemastraat. Map p 104.

Paradiso LEIDSEPLEIN   An old church has been transformed into this majestic club, with lofty ceilings and high balconies encircling the dance floor. Big-name DJs and theme nights help make this place appealing to a variety of stylish people. *Weteringschans 6–8.* ☎ *020/626-4521. www.paradiso.nl. Cover 8€–22€. Tram: 1, 2, 5, 7, or 10 to Leidseplein. Map p 104.*

★★ Tonight OOST   The city's hottest club is in the ultratrendy Hotel Arena. Talented DJs keep everybody happy with a mix of music from the '60s to the '90s. A youngish, well-dressed crowd flocks here, especially on weekends after midnight. *'s-Gravesandestraat 51.* ☎ *020/850-2451. www.hotelarena.nl. Cover 6€–10€. Tram: 7 or 10 to Korte 's-Gravesandestraat. Map p 104.*

Gay & Lesbian
Amstel FiftyFour REMBRANDT-PLEIN   One of Amsterdam's most venerable gay bars, on gay-friendly Amstel, has had a makeover, changing it from a cozily old-fashioned place to one which, if not exactly hip, has a definite sense of style. It remains engagingly convivial, though, and the regulars will occasionally break into song. *Amstel*

54. ☎ *020/623-4254. www.amstel fiftyfour.nl. Tram: 4, 9, or 14 to Rembrandtplein. Map p 104.*

★ Exit OLD CENTER   On a street that has no shortage of gay venues, Exit stands out for having some of the best DJs in town, who spin up a pounding mix of techno, progressive house, and hip-hop for a hot-to-trot 20s and up crowd that runs from regular guys to fashion queens. There's an attached cafe. *Reguliers-dwarsstraat 42.* ☎ *020/638-5700. www.clubexit.eu. Cover 10€–15€. Tram: 1, 2, or 5 to Koningsplein. Map p 104.*

Saarein JORDAAN   This cafe is a longtime favorite with lesbians, though it's increasingly drawing a mixed crowd. A great location in the Jordaan makes it appealing to locals. Convivial atmosphere. *Elandsstraat 119.* ☎ *020/623-4901. www.saarein. nl. Tram: 7, 10, or 17 to Marnixstraat. Map p 104.*

★ Soho OLD CENTER   The city's quintessential gay pub, open until 3am Monday to Thursday, 4am Friday and Saturday, and midnight Sunday, doesn't really get going until late (after 11pm). *Reguliersd-warsstraat 36.* ☎ *020/638-5700. www.pubsoho.eu. Tram: 1, 2, or 5 to Koningsplein. Map p 104.*

★ Vive-la-Vie REMBRANDTPLEIN   Open for more than 25 years, this

The scene at luxe Jimmy Woo smolders late into the night.

Order a colaatje pils (co-la-che pilss) if you want beer in a small glass, or a bakkie or vaas if you'd like a large.

cafe is the place for lesbians in Amsterdam. The crowd is young and lively, and lipstick isn't forbidden. Very popular in the early evenings. *Amstelstraat 7.* ☎ *020/624-0114.*

www.vivelavie.net. Tram: 4, 9, or 14 to Rembrandtplein. Map p 104.

Pubs

O'Donnell's Irish Pub PIJP   This neighborhood Irish pub pulls in many of the young, up-and-coming professionals who live in the Pijp. It's a happy, boisterous place where the Guinness is good and the bartenders are Irish and friendly. The down-to-earth food—Guinness stew, fish and chips, grilled lamb chops—is excellent. *Ferdinand Bolstraat 5 (at Marie Heinekenplein).* ☎ *020/676-7786. Tram: 16 or 24 to Stadhouderskade. Map p 103.*

Three Sisters Grand Pub LEIDSEPLEIN   Popular with the throngs of visiting Brits, this is a good place to come for a pint of English lager or warm ale. Especially busy for happy hour. *Leidseplein 2.* ☎ *020/428-0428. Tram: 1, 2, 5, 7, or 10 to Leidseplein. Map p 104.* ●

Cannabis *Tolerance*

Amsterdam's reputation as a wild party town is a direct result of its *tolerance* toward cannabis. But the practice is technically illegal and only just tolerated. Local producers are allowed to operate so long as they don't go in for large-scale production (some of their wares are used for pain relief). Individuals are allowed to be in possession of up to 30 grams (1 oz.) for personal use, but can only purchase 5 grams (about ⅙ oz.) at a time. "Coffee shops" in Amsterdam are not places to get a meal, they're places where a customer can purchase marijuana or hashish. They are licensed and controlled and provide a place where patrons can sit and smoke all day if they so choose—and the coffee actually is not bad. Coffee shops are not allowed to sell alcohol, and only some serve food (usually very light snacks). Warmoesstraat, on the fringe of the Red Light District, is lined with coffee shops, making it the prime spot for coffee-shop crawls by bands of young tourists looking for a good time (they're usually dazed by the end of the evening, as you can imagine, so things are actually quite mellow). One of the friendlier places is Coffeeshop Sheeba, Warmoesstraat 73 (☎ 020/512-3127), open daily 9am to 1am.

Arts & Entertainment
Best Bets

★ Best **Place for Laughing the Night Away**
Boom Chicago, *Leidseplein 12* (p 116)

Best **Chamber Orchestra**
★★ Netherlands Chamber Orchestra, Beurs van Berlage, *Beursplein 1* (p 116)

Best for **Controversial Movies**
De Balie, *Kleine-Gartmanplantsoen 10* (p 117)

Best **Acoustics**
★★★ Concertgebouw, *Concertgebouwplein 2–6* (p 116)

Best **Contemporary Concert Space**
★ Heineken Music Hall, *ArenA Blvd. 590* (p 117)

Best for **Opera**
★★★ Muziektheater, *Waterlooplein 22* (p 117)

Best for **Gay & Lesbian Plays**
★ Melkweg, *Lijnbaansgracht 234A* (p 120)

Best for **Lavish Musicals**
★ Carré, *Amstel 115–125* (p 120)

Best for **Ballet**
★★★ Muziektheater, *Waterlooplein 22* (p 117)

Best for **Modern Dutch Theater**
★ Stadsschouwburg, *Leidseplein 26* (p 120)

Best **Blues Venue**
Maloe Melo, *Lijnbaansgracht 163* (p 118)

Best for **Experimental Music**
★★ Muziekgebouw aan 't IJ, *Piet Heinkade 1* (p 117)

Best **Free Concerts**
★ Vondelpark Openluchttheater, *Vondelpark* (p 117)

Previous page: A performance at the highly regarded National Ballet.
This page: The Muziektheater.

Museum District **A&E**

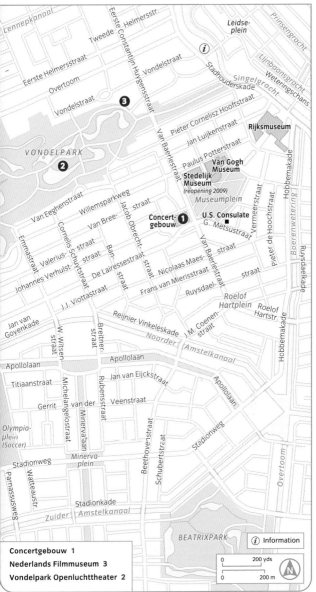

Concertgebouw **1**

Nederlands Filmmuseum **3**

Vondelpark Openluchttheater **2**

i Information

0   200 yds

0   200 m

Central Amsterdam **A&E**

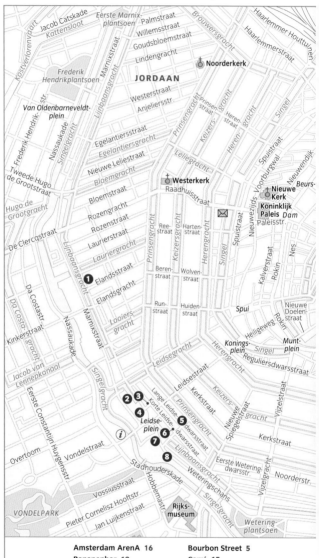

Amsterdam ArenA 16
Bananenbar 12
Beurs van Berlage 9
Bimhuis 11
Boom Chicago 3

Bourbon Street 5
Carré 15
Casa Rosso 13
De Balie 7
Heineken Music Hall 17

Jazz Café Alto 6
Maloe Melo 1
Melkweg 2
Muziekgebouw
  aan 't IJ 10

Muziektheater 14
Paradiso 8
Stadsschouwburg 4

Arts & Entertainment A to Z

Classical Music

★★ Beurs van Berlage OLD CEN-TER   The former home of the Amsterdam Stock Exchange (built in 1903) is now a congress and sometime concert venue with two halls. It's home to the Netherlands Philharmonic Orchestra (which performs most of its local concerts at the Concertgebouw) and the Netherlands Chamber Orchestra (most concerts are performed at other venues around the city). *Beursplein 1.* ☎ *020/ 521-7520. www.berlage.com. Tickets 15€–75€. Tram: 4, 9, 14, 16, 24, or 25 to the Dam. Map p 114.*

★★★ Concertgebouw MUSEUM DISTRICT   The Concert Building, home of the Royal Concertgebouw Orchestra, first opened its doors in 1888 and is touted as one of the most acoustically perfect concert halls in the world. The world's greatest orchestras, ensembles, conductors, and soloists regularly perform here. There are two halls, a main hall and a recital hall, which hosts smaller ensembles, like chamber orchestras. Each hall hosts a daily performance, making the venue one of the busiest concert halls in the world. *Concertgebouwplein 2–6.* ☎ *020/671-8345. www.concert gebouw.nl. Tickets 15€–100€; Aug*

Musicians rehearse at the Muziekgebouw aan 't IJ.

summer concerts 30€. Tram: 3, 5, 12, 16, or 24 to Museumplein. Map p 113.

Comedy Theater

★ Boom Chicago LEIDSEPLEIN   Amsterdam's premier comedy theater has been going strong since 1993, with lots of improvisational shows. Most performances are in English. Good fun. *Leidseplein Theater, Leidseplein 12.* ☎ *020/530-7310. www.boomchicago.nl. Tickets 15€–35€. Tram: 1, 2, 5, 6, 7, or 10 to Leidseplein. Map p 114.*

A performance at the Concertgebouw.

Concerts

Amsterdam ArenA ZUIDOOST
From sports (soccer, mostly) to big-name rock concerts, the city's biggest events take place at this giant arena, located in southeast Amsterdam. *ArenA Blvd. 1, Amsterdam-Zuidoost.* ☎ *020/311-1313. www.amsterdamarena.nl. Tickets 15€–60€. Metro: Bijlmer/ArenA. Map p 114.*

★ **Heineken Music Hall**
ZUIDOOST   Near the giant Amsterdam ArenA, the smaller Heineken Music Hall hosts more intimate concerts. Performers have included Avril Lavigne, Alanis Morissette, Duran Duran, the Black Eyed Peas, Michael Bolton, Marilyn Manson, and Meat Loaf, among others. *ArenA Blvd. 590* ☎ *0900/6874-24255. www.heineken-music-hall.nl. Tickets 30€–75€. Metro: Bijlmer/ArenA. Map p 114.*

★★ **Muziekgebouw aan 't IJ**
WATERFRONT   The city's newest concert hall opened in 2005 just east of Centraal Station. It's the hub of contemporary and experimental music in Amsterdam, featuring top local and international musicians. See "Bimhuis," below. *Piet Heinkade 1.* ☎ *020/788-2000. www.muziekge bouw.nl. Tickets 10€–60€. Tram: 25 or 26 to Muziekgebouw/Bimhuis. Map p 114.*

Paradiso LEIDSEPLEIN   This old church has been transformed to present an eclectic variety of music. It's a great place for dance events Thursday through Sunday, and it doubles as a concert venue for big-name artists. The Rolling Stones, David Bowie, and Prince have all played here. *Weteringschans 6–8.* ☎ *020/626-4521. www.paradiso.nl. Tickets 8€–22€. Tram: 1, 2, 5, 7, or 10 to Leidseplein. Map p 114.*

★ **Vondelpark Openlucht-theater** MUSEUM DISTRICT   This open-air venue comes to life on

The National Ballet and Netherlands Dance Theater, both highly regarded, perform at the Muziektheater.

certain nights during July and August, when pop, rock, Latin, or classical artists give free concerts in the midst of peaceful, green Vondelpark. Bring a picnic and enjoy an enchanting evening under the stars. *Vondelpark.* ☎ *020/428-3360. www. openluchttheater.nl. Free admission. Tram: 1, 2, 5, 7, or 10 to Leidseplein. Map p 113.*

Dance & Opera

★★★ **Muziektheater** WATERLOOPLEIN   One of the city's stellar performance venues has a superbly equipped 1,600-seat auditorium and is the home base of the highly regarded Netherlands Opera and National Ballet. The acclaimed Netherlands Dance Theater, based in The Hague, also performs here regularly. *Waterlooplein 22 (theater entrance Amstel 3)* ☎ *020/625-5455. www.hetmuziektheater.nl. Tickets 20€–90€. Tram: 9 or 14 to Waterlooplein. Map p 114.*

Film

De Balie LEIDSEPLEIN   This all-purpose cultural center has an eclectic calendar of workshops, lectures, and film festivals. You can see controversial and award-winning features and documentaries and lots of interesting movies from around the world that don't make it to mainstream theaters. *Kleine-Gartmanplantsoen 10.* ☎ *020/553-5151. www.debalie.nl. Movie tickets 8€; lectures 6€–10€. Tram: 1, 2, 5, 7, or 10 to Leidseplein. Map p 114.*

★ Nederlands Filmmuseum

MUSEUM DISTRICT   Much more than just a museum, this striking venue is located inside the magnificent Vondelpark and features two theaters (one of them with a fabulous Art Deco interior) that schedule interesting retrospectives and film festivals. *Vondelpark.* ☎ *020/589-1400. www.filmmuseum.nl. Tickets 8€. Tram: 1, 2, 5, 7, or 10 to Leidseplein. Map p 113.*

Jazz

★ Bimhuis   WATERFRONT   Next

door to the Muziekgebouw aan 't IJ (see above), this is the city's premier jazz, blues, and improvisational venue. *Piet Heinkade 3.* ☎ *020/788-2188. www.bimhuis.nl. Tickets 10€–30€. Tram: 25 or 26 to Muziekgebouw/Bimhuis. Map p 114.*

Bourbon Street LEIDSEPLEIN   In this intimate cafe, you'll find excellent local jazz, blues, soul, and funk. Well-known groups from the U.S. and Europe play here, too. This place is hopping until well after midnight. *Leidsekruisstraat 6–8.*

☎ *020/623-3440. www.bourbon street.nl. Cover 10€ for special acts. Tram: 1, 2, 5, 7, or 10 to Leidseplein. Map p 114.*

Jazz Café Alto LEIDSEPLEIN   Top-notch quartets play nightly in this small cafe, with the occasional blues band mixed in. On some Wednesday evenings the noted local saxophonists Hans Dulfer and his daughter Candy Dulfer play. *Korte Leidsedwarsstraat 115.* ☎ *020/626-3249. www.jazz-cafe-alto.nl. No cover. Tram: 1, 2, 5, 7, or 10 to Leidseplein. Map p 114.*

Maloe Melo JORDAAN   This small club presents live blues most nights, interspersed with evenings of jazz and country, and jams on Tuesday and Thursday nights. Big-name musicians are featured occasionally as well. *Lijnbaansgracht 163.* ☎ *020/420-4592. www.maloe melo.nl. Cover 5€. Tram: 7, 10, or 17 to Elandsgracht. Map p 114.*

Sex Shows

Bananenbar OLD CENTER Bananas are the featured props in the nightly sex shows here. The audience (which tends toward hormone-driven young men) is encouraged to participate. *Oudezijds Achterburgwal 37.* ☎ *020/622-4670. www.bananenbar.com. Cover 30€,*

The Filmmuseum shows a wide variety of films throughout the year, including some English-language films.

Jazz lovers have a number of excellent venues to choose from in Amsterdam.

or 45€ including all drinks. *Tram: 1, 2, 4, 5, 9, 13, 16, 17, 24, 25, or 26 to Centraal Station. Map p 114.*

Casa Rosso OLD CENTER   In its own words, Casa Rosso puts on "one of the most superior Erotic shows in the world, with a tremendous choreography and a high-level cast." You

may not describe it in those words, but this live sex show joint is very popular with throngs of visiting young men. *Oudezijds Achterburgwal 106–108.* ☎ *020/627-8943. www.bananenbar.com. Cover 45€, including all drinks. Tram: 4, 9, 14, 16, 24, or 25 to the Dam. Map p 114.*

Buying Tickets

The most convenient ticket outlet in the city is the Amsterdam **Uit Buro (AUB) Ticketshop** located at Leidseplein 26 (☎ 0900/0191; www.aub.nl; tram: 1, 2, 5, 7, or 10). Here you can reserve and purchase tickets for any venue in town and also pick up a plethora of brochures, pamphlets, and schedules for any cultural event in Amsterdam, including film festivals and temporary exhibits at galleries and museums. There's a charge of 2€ to 3€ per ticket, but you may consider it worth the time you'll save by not having to chase down tickets on your own. This office also allows you to purchase tickets and make reservations before leaving home via their website. For phone reservations using a credit card, AUB is open daily from 9am to 9pm. The office itself is open Monday to Wednesday and Saturday from 10am to 6pm, Thursday from 10am to 9pm, and Sunday from noon to 6pm.

The **VVV Amsterdam** tourist information office (p 166) can also reserve tickets, but it usually has a longer wait time and the charge is 2.50€ per ticket. If you are staying at an upmarket hotel, I suggest calling the concierge (even before you leave home) to arrange for reservations.

The Carré theater hosts lavish productions of Dutch plays as well as top Broadway and London shows.

Theater

★ **Carré** OOST This big, plush theater used to be a full-time circus arena. Now it hosts the most lavish Dutch-language (and some English) productions of top Broadway and London musicals such as *Les Miserables* and *Miss Saigon*. Several international opera, modern dance, and ballet companies also perform here on occasion. *Amstel 115–125.*

Stadsschouwburg.

☎ *0900/252-5255. www.theater carre.nl. Tickets 15€–125€. Tram: 7 or 10 to Weesperplein. Map p 114.*

★ **Melkweg** LEIDSEPLEIN This large contemporary multidimensional venue includes a theater, cinema, concert hall, photo gallery, and exhibition space. Its theater tends to showcase new groups, both international and local, with emphasis on experimentalism. Comedy, multicultural, and gay and lesbian plays are staged here, too. Most performances are in Dutch. *Lijnbaansgracht 234A.* ☎ *020/531-8181. www.melkweg.nl. Tickets 5€–10€. Tram: 1, 2, 5, 7, or 10 to Leidseplein. Map p 114.*

★ **Stadsschouwburg** LEIDSE-PLEIN This 950-seat municipal theater is the city's main venue for mainstream Dutch theater and the occasional play in English, both classic and modern. Opera and ballet performances are also occasionally staged here. *Leidseplein 26.* ☎ *020/624-2311. www.stadsschouwburg amsterdam.nl. Tickets 10€–45€. Tram: 1, 2, 5, 7, or 10 to Leidseplein. Map p 114.* ●

9 The Best **Lodging**

Lodging **Best Bets**

Best for **John Lennon Fans**
★ Hilton Amsterdam $$$ Apollo-laan 138 (p 128)

Best for **Sleeping on a Houseboat**
★ Acacia $$ Lindengracht 251 (p 126)

Best for **Business Travelers**
★ Renaissance Amsterdam $$$ Kattengat 1 (p 132)

Best **When Money Is No Object**
★★★ Hotel de l'Europe $$$$ Nieuwe Doelenstraat 2–8 (p 129)

Best for **Affordable Minimalist Design**
★ Arena $$'s-Gravesandestraat 51 (p 129)

Best **Boutique Hotel**
★★ The Dylan $$$$ Keizersgracht 384 (p 128)

Best **Location for Families**
Eden Lancaster $$ Plantage Middenlaan 48 (p 128)

Best **Indoor Pool**
★★★ Amstel InterContinental Amsterdam $$$$ Professor Tulpplein 1 (p 126)

Best for **Young Party Animals**
Winston $ Warmoesstraat 129 (p 134)

Best **Place to Call Home**
★ Vondelpark Museum B&B $ Vossiusstraat 14 (p 134)

Best **Hotel Gym**
★ Marriott $$$ Stadhouderskade 12 (p 130)

Best **Romantic Getaway**
★★ Pulitzer $$$$ Prinsengracht 315–331 (p 131)

Best **Minimalist Interior Design**
★★ Lloyd $–$$$$ Handels-kade 34 (p 129)

Best **Affordable Hotel with Elegant Rooms**
★ Piet Hein $$ Vossiusstraat 52–53 (p 131)

Best for **Shopaholics**
★★ Patou $$$ Pieter Cornelisz Hooftstraat 63 (p 131)

Best for **Cultivating the Mental Faculties**
★★ De Filosoof $$ Anna van den Vondelstraat 6 (p 127)

Previous page: Quality accommodations abound in this lively city. This page: The Agora.

Museum District **Lodging**

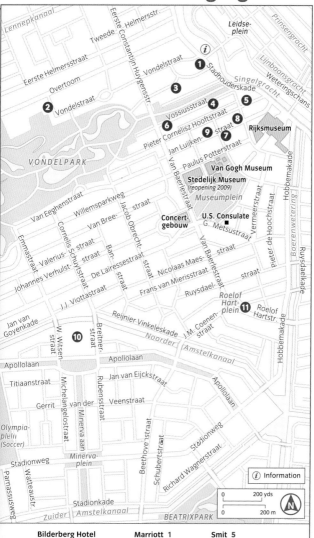

Central Amsterdam **Lodging**

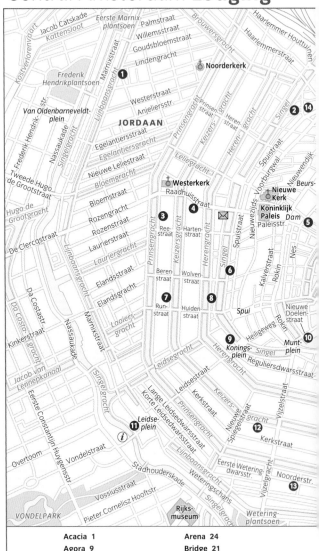

Acacia 1

Agora 9

Ambassade 8

Amstel InterContinental
Amsterdam 22

Amsterdam American 11

Arena 24

Bridge 21

Budget Hotel Clemens 4

The Dylan 7

Eden Hotel Amsterdam 18

Eden Lancaster 23

| Information | Main Post Office | Metro |

Hoksbergen 6
Hotel de l'Europe 10
Keizershof 12
Lloyd 15
Mercure Amsterdam
    Arthur Frommer 13

NH Grand Hotel
    Krasnapolsky 5
Prinsenhof 20
Pulitzer 3
Radisson SAS 17

Renaissance
    Amsterdam 14
Seven Bridges 19
Singel 2
Winston 16

Amsterdam Hotels A to Z

★ **Acacia** JORDAAN Simple, clean rooms, friendly owners, and a good location (on a canal close to trendy restaurants) make this small hotel a decent bet. All rooms have canal views, but there's no elevator. For an authentic Amsterdam living experience, rent one of the hotel's two nearby houseboats. *Lindengracht 251.* ☎ *020/622-1460. www.hotel acacia.nl. 16 units, including 2 houseboats. Doubles 80€–90€ w/breakfast; houseboat 95€–110€ w/breakfast. MC, V. Tram: 3 or 10 to Marnixplein. Map p 124.*

Agora CANAL BELT Great location and friendly service make this small hotel a good value. Rooms are small (except for family rooms, which are quite spacious) and are outfitted with mahogany and antiques. Rooms overlooking the canal can be somewhat noisy, so if you're a light sleeper, ask for a room in back, with views of a pretty garden. There's no elevator. *Singel 462.* ☎ *20/627-2200. www.hotelagora.nl. 16 units. Doubles 99€–159€ w/breakfast. AE, DC, MC, V. Tram: 1, 2, or 5 to Koningsplein. Map p 124.*

★ **Ambassade Hotel** CANAL BELT Ten elegant 17th- and 18th-century canal houses have been renovated to create this perfectly located gem. Individually decorated rooms are furnished in Louis XV and XVI styles. You'll find free Internet and bike rental on the premises. Not all rooms are accessible by elevator, so be sure to specify your needs when booking. *Herengracht 341.* ☎ *020/555-0222. www.ambassade-hotel.nl. 59 units. Doubles 195€–275€. AE, DC, MC, V. Tram: 1, 2, or 5 to Spui. Map p 124.*

★★★ **Amstel InterContinental Amsterdam** OOST The grande dame of Dutch hotels since its opening in 1867 is still top-notch both in luxurious accommodations and superior customer service. Plush, elegant rooms come with Italian-marble bathrooms. There's a gorgeous indoor pool alongside the modern health club, with steam room and sauna. The hotel's restaurant, La Rive (p 98), is one of the best in the city. *Professor Tulpplein 1.* ☎ *020/622-6060. www.ichotels group.com. 79 units. Doubles 510€–620€. AE, DC, MC, V. Tram: 7 or 10 to Weesperplein. Map p 124.*

Sleeping quarters in one of the Acacia's houseboat rooms.

One of the Bilderberg Hotel Jan Luyken's sophisticated, modern rooms.

★★ Amsterdam American Hotel LEIDSEPLEIN A fanciful, castlelike mix of Venetian Gothic and Art Nouveau, the American has been both a prominent landmark and a popular meeting place for Amsterdammers since 1900. Rooms are subdued, refined, and superbly furnished. Some have views of the Singelgracht canal, while others overlook kaleidoscopic Leidseplein. *Leidsekade 97.* ☎ *020/556-3000. www.amsterdamamerican.com. 175 units. Doubles 120€–280€. AE, DC, MC, V. Tram: 1, 2, 5, 7, or 10 to Leidseplein. Map p 125.*

★ Bilderberg Hotel Jan Luyken MUSEUM DISTRICT Steps from the Rijksmuseum, this charming small hotel is located on a leafy residential street. The attractive rooms feature a sophisticated, modern decor and are meticulously maintained. With amenities such as 24-hour room service and in-room massage, this place feels like a large, full-service hotel without the crowds. *Jan Luijkenstraat 58.* ☎ *020/573-0730. www.janluyken.nl. 62 units. Doubles 129€–159€. AE, DC, MC, V. Tram: 2 or 5 to Hobbemastraat. Map p 123.*

★ Bridge OOST The riverfront location and large, simply furnished but comfortable rooms make this hotel a great value. Two airy and spacious apartments with large picture windows are great for families. The full Dutch breakfast served every morning is a nice touch. *Amstel 107–111.* ☎ *020/623-7068. www. thebridgehotel.nl. 43 units. Doubles 115€–170€ w/breakfast. AE, DC, MC, V. Tram: 7 or 10 to Weesperplein. Map p 124.*

Budget Hotel Clemens JORDAAN This small, tidy hotel is operated by a mother-daughter team who take personal care of the comfortable rooms. Nos. 7 and 8 have balconies facing the Westerkerk. *Raadhuisstraat 39.* ☎ *020/624-6089. www.clemenshotel.nl. 9 units, 5 with bathroom. Doubles 75€–120€. AE, MC, V. Tram: 13, 14, or 17 to Westerkerk. Map p 124.*

★★ The College MUSEUM DISTRICT This modern boutique hotel is housed in a former school building, thus the name. It's just a short walk from the major museums. Expect to see plenty of trendy 30-something European professionals here. *Roelof Hartstraat 1.* ☎ *020/571-1511. www.collegehotelamsterdam.com. 43 units. Doubles 180€–250€. AE, DC, MC, V. Tram: 3, 5, 12, or 24 to Roelof Hartplein. Map p 123.*

★★ De Filosoof MUSEUM DISTRICT In a leafy and upscale residential neighborhood not far from Vondelpark, you'll find this small, friendly hotel. Rooms are small but charming, and some are very bright, with large wood-framed windows. They're individually decorated in themes that reflect various philosophies (like the Golden Age–style Spinoza room, or the simply decorated Thoreau room). A great value, especially if you want peace and quiet. It's about a 10-minute walk to the center of the city. *Anna van den Vondelstraat 6.* ☎ *020/683-3013. www.hotelfilosoof.nl. 38 units. Doubles 105€–155€ w/breakfast. AE, MC, V. Tram: 1 to Jan Pieter Heijestraat. Map p 123.*

★★ **The Dylan** CANAL BELT   Amsterdam's most lavish boutique hotel is set in a 17th-century building on one of the city's most scenic canals. Modern elegance reigns here, with four-poster beds and spacious bathrooms. Each room is individually decorated with rich fabrics and bold colors. Service is superb and discreet enough for celebrities. *Keizersgracht 384.* ☎ *020/530-2010. www.dylan amsterdam.com. 41 units. Doubles 455€–560€. AE, DC, MC, V. Tram: 1, 2, or 5 to Spui. Map p 124.*

★ **Eden Hotel Amsterdam** OLD CENTER   Across the Amstel from the Muziektheater (p 117), this scenically sited hotel has bright, modern, recently renovated rooms. Some are more spacious than others, and those with river views are the best of the bunch and the most in demand. *Amstel 144.* ☎ *020/530-7888. www. edenamsterdamhotel.com. 218 units. Doubles 175€–200€. AE, DC, MC, V.*

The Manhattan suite at the Dylan.

A suite at the College.

Tram: 4 or 9 to Rembrandtplein. Map p 124.

kids **Eden Lancaster** OOST   A stone's throw from Artis Zoo, this is a great location for families, away from the hustle and bustle of the old center, but just a 10-minute tram ride or 30-minute walk away. The quietest neighborhood in Amsterdam is also a short walk from the Tropenmuseum and the Botanical Gardens. Attractive triple rooms are perfect if you're traveling with kids. *Plantage Middenlaan 48.* ☎ *020/ 535-6888. www.edenhotelgroup. com. 91 units. Doubles 130€–175€. AE, DC, MC, V. Tram: 9 or 14 to Plantage Kerklaan. Map p 124.*

★ **Hilton Amsterdam** NIEUW ZUID   The infamous room 902 is

where John Lennon and Yoko Ono had their "Bed in for Peace" in 1969. The designers of the hotel consulted Yoko when renovating the room, and it now features extensive use of natural materials only. Modern facilities and a good location, within walking distance from the Rijksmuseum. *Apollolaan 138.* ☎ *020/710-6000. www.amsterdam.hilton.com. 271 units. Doubles 225€–325€. AE, DC, MC, V. Tram: 5 or 24 to Apollolaan. Map p 123.*

Hoksbergen CANAL BELT This attractive budget hotel is housed in a 300-year-old canal house and offers small but bright and (very) clean rooms at affordable rates. Rooms at the front have canal views. There's no elevator. *Singel 301.* ☎ *020/626-6043. www.hotelhoksbergen.com. 14 units. Doubles 72€–125€ w/breakfast. AE, DC, MC, V. Tram: 1, 2, or 5 to Spui. Map p 124.*

★ **Hotel Arena** OOST What used to be an orphanage dating back to 1890 is now a stylish hotel catering mostly to European yuppies who love the spare modern rooms, each individually decorated by up-and-coming Dutch designers. There's a casual eatery called To Dine and a bar called To Drink. The hotel's hot nightclub, Tonight (p 109), is housed in the old orphanage chapel. *'s-Gravesandestraat 51.* ☎ *020/850-2410. www.hotelarena.nl. 121 units. Doubles 100€–175€ w/breakfast. AE, DC, MC, V. Tram: 7 or 10 to Korte 's-Gravesandestraat. Map p 124.*

★★★ **Hotel de l'Europe** OLD CENTER This classic luxury hotel, a member of the Leading Hotels of the World, commands a prime riverside location. The rooms are plush, spacious, and bright, and all boast marble bathrooms. There are two highly acclaimed restaurants (including Excelsior, p 97) and a summer terrace overlooking the Amstel.

Nieuwe Doelenstraat 2–8. ☎ *020/531-1777. www.leurope.nl. 100 units. Doubles 420€–510€. AE, DC, MC, V. Tram: 4, 9, 14, 16, 24, or 25 to De Munt. Map p 124.*

Keizershof CANAL BELT This four-story canal house dates back to 1672. A grand piano in the hotel's lounge adds a certain stateliness to the place. Rooms are beamed and cozy with simple, modern furnishings, but only two have private bathrooms. In summer you can enjoy a delicious Dutch breakfast in the flower-filled courtyard. There's no elevator. *Keizersgracht 618.* ☎ *020/622-2855. www.hotelkeizershof.nl. 4 units, 2 with bathroom. Doubles with bathroom 90€–110€; doubles without bathroom 80€; all w/breakfast. MC, V. Tram: 16, 24, or 25 to Keizersgracht. Map p 124.*

★★ **Lloyd Hotel** WATERFRONT This historic Amsterdam School–style hotel in the up-and-coming Eastern Docklands neighborhood boasts a wide variety of rooms—from basic to luxury. Choose from tiny rooms without baths to impressive suites and duplexes (one even has a grand piano and a sweeping

The Hotel Arena's rooms feature sleek, modern design.

staircase). Most rooms are outfitted by contemporary Dutch architects and designers. There's an excellent restaurant on the premises. *Oostelijke Handelskade 34.* ☎ *020/561-3636. www.lloydhotel.com. 117 units, 106 with bathroom. Doubles with bathroom 140€–450€; doubles without bathroom 95€. AE, DC, MC, V. Tram: 10 or 26 to Rietlandpark. Map p 124.*

★ **Marriott** LEIDSEPLEIN Commanding a fantastic location between Leidseplein and Vondelpark, this Marriott has been meticulously renovated with firm mattresses, fluffy comforters, and a new gym featuring the latest workout equipment. The staff goes out of their way to provide for your comfort, and the concierge is a great source of help for both tourist and business information. *Stadhouderskade 12.* ☎ *020/607-5555. www.marriott.com. 392 units. Doubles 225€–395€. AE, DC, MC, V. Tram: 1, 2, 5, 7, or 10 to Leidseplein. Map p 123.*

Mercure Amsterdam Arthur Frommer CANAL BELT This small, friendly hotel once owned by Arthur Frommer is tucked away off Vijzelgracht. The rooms are not huge but are very stylish, with soft pastel colors. There's a cozy bar.

One of the Lloyd's basic rooms.

Noorderstraat 46. ☎ *020/622-0328. www.accorhotels.com. 92 units. Doubles 125€–170€. AE, DC, MC, V. Tram: 16, 24, or 25 to Prinsengracht. Map p 124.*

Museumzicht MUSEUM DISTRICT This basic hotel is housed in a Victorian house just across from the Rijksmuseum. Rooms are small but clean, decorated with an eclectic mix of antique furnishings. There's no elevator and the steps are quite steep. *Jan Luijkenstraat 22.* ☎ *020/ 671-2954. www.hotelmuseumzicht.nl.*

Hotel de l'Europe's impressive exterior.

A Canal-House Warning

Elevators are difficult things to shoehorn into the cramped confines of a 17th-century canal house and cost more than some moderately priced and budget hotels can afford. Many simply don't have them. If lugging your old wooden sea chest up six flights of steep, narrow, hard-to-navigate stairs is liable to void your life insurance, better make sure an elevator is in place and working. Should there be no such amenity and you have trouble climbing stairs, ask for a room on a low floor.

14 units, 3 with bathroom. Doubles with bathroom 98€; doubles without bathroom 78€; all w/breakfast. AE, DC, MC, V. Tram: 2 or 5 to Hobbemastraat. Map p 123.

NH Grand Hotel Krasnapolsky
OLD CENTER Smack in the midst of it all, the "Kras" (as it's known locally) faces the Royal Palace and is an Amsterdam landmark. The sizes and shapes of the rooms vary considerably and the upkeep on them is variable. Renovations are progressing somewhat haphazardly; ask for a newly renovated room when you make your reservation. Dam 9. ☎ 020/554-9111. www.nh-hotels. com. 468 units. Doubles 161€–207€. AE, DC, MC, V. Tram: 4, 9, 14, 16, 24, or 25 to the Dam. Map p 124.

Owl Hotel MUSEUM DISTRICT
This solid bargain choice is just a few minutes' walk from Leidseplein, but in a quiet spot. Rooms are fairly compact, with oak furnishings and whitewashed walls. There's a bar and a small garden, great for lounging on a warm summer day. Roemer Visscherstraat 1. ☎ 020/618-9484. www.owl-hotel.nl. 34 units. Doubles 105€–130€ w/breakfast. AE, DC, MC, V. Tram: 1 to Stadhouderskade. Map p 123.

★ **Patou** MUSEUM DISTRICT
Smack in the middle of the city's

most elegant shopping street, this small boutique hotel goes beyond offering mere style—innovative though the minimalist design is. Patou keeps a laserlike focus on doing good by its guests. Pieter Cornelisz Hooftstraat 63. ☎ 020/676-0232. www.hotelpatou.nl. 12 units. Doubles 175€–235€. AE, DC, MC, V. Tram: 2 or 5 to Hobbemastraat. Map p 123.

★ **Piet Hein** MUSEUM DISTRICT
The most modern and attractive reasonably priced hotel in Amsterdam boasts a refreshing "nautical" decor in all of its stylish rooms. The deluxe rooms—located in a recently renovated wing of the hotel—come with air-conditioning, which is unusual for a hotel in this price range. There's a comfortable bar/lounge where you can unwind in the evenings. Vossiusstraat 52–53. ☎ 020/662-7205. www.hotelpiethein.com. 65 units. Doubles 120€–195€ w/breakfast. AE, DC, MC, V. Tram: 3, 5, or 12 to Van Baerlestraat. Map p 123.

Prinsenhof CANAL BELT This recently renovated canal house offers basic but comfortable rooms with beamed ceilings. Front rooms look out onto the Prinsengracht, where colorful houseboats are moored. There's no elevator, but a pulley hauls your luggage up and down the stairs. Prinsengracht 810.

☎ *020/623-1772. www.hotelprinsen hof.com. 10 units, 4 with bathroom. Doubles with bathroom 85€; doubles without bathroom 65€; all w/breakfast. AE, MC, V. Tram: 4 to Prinsengracht. Map p 124.*

★ **Pulitzer** CANAL BELT   The Pulitzer offers its lucky guests pure luxury without being ostentatious. A superior location on a canal at the edge of the Jordaan, rooms so plush you sink into them, and a fantastic restaurant (p 99) make this a good place to splurge on a romantic getaway. *Prinsengracht 315–331. ☎ 020/ 523-5235. www.starwoodhotels.com. 230 units. Doubles 475€–555€. AE, DC, MC, V. Tram: 13, 14, or 17 to Westermarkt. Map p 124.*

★★ **Radisson SAS** OLD CENTER This sprawling hotel is close to everything. There are four room categories, so be sure to state your preference when you reserve. The Dutch rooms come with oak furnishings and orange curtains; the Scandinavian, Asian, and Art Deco rooms are sparser and airier. The hotel has a full restaurant and a bar that serves light meals. *Rusland 17. ☎ 020/623-1231. www.radissonsas.com. 242 units. Doubles 240€–350€. AE, DC, MC, V. Tram: 4, 9, 14, 16, 24, or 25 to Spui. Map p 124.*

★ **Renaissance Amsterdam** OLD CENTER   The Renaissance is a standout among the city's large business hotels, tucked away off a charming canal just a 5-minute walk from Centraal Station. It feels much cozier than you'd expect from its size. Rooms are very spacious, with picture windows and large bathrooms. Staff go out of their way to help. *Kattengat 1. ☎ 020/621-2223. www.marriott.com. 381 units. Doubles 149€–345€. AE, DC, MC, V. Tram: 1, 2, 5, 13, or 17 to Martelaarsgracht. Map p 124.*

★★ **Seven Bridges** CANAL BELT This canal-house gem is meticulously maintained. Each individually decorated room boasts antique furnishings (Art Deco, Biedermeier, Louis XVI, rococo), handmade Italian drapes, and wood-tiled floors. Attic

The cozy bar at the Pulitzer.

A room at the Renaissance Amsterdam.

rooms have sloped ceilings and exposed wood beams. *Reguliersgracht 31.* ☎ *020/623-1329. 11 units. Doubles 100€–260€ w/breakfast. AE, MC, V. Tram: 4 to Keizersgracht. Map p 124.*

Singel Hotel CANAL BELT   Three canal houses were united to create this bright and welcoming hotel, conveniently located near Centraal Station. A few of the modern, spacious rooms have an attractive view of the Singel canal. *Singel 13–17.* ☎ *020/ 626-3108. www.singelhotel.nl. 32 units. Doubles 120€–160€ w/breakfast. AE, DC, MC, V. Tram: 1, 2, 5, 13, or 17 to Martelaarsgracht. Map p 124.*

Smit MUSEUM DISTRICT   Steps from all the elegant shops on P.C. Hooftstraat, this hotel offers comfortable, if slightly small, rooms at a

Money-Saving Tips

Amsterdam's hotels can be expensive. There are around 30,000 hotel and hostel beds available, 40% of which are in four- and five-star hotels. The Netherlands adheres to the Benelux Hotel Classification System, which awards stars to hotels based on set criteria   having a pool, an elevator, and so forth. The hotel with the most stars is not necessarily the most comfortable or elegant (though often it is). Each establishment must display a sign indicating its classification, from "1" for those with minimum amenities to "5" for deluxe, full-service hotels. The city has moved in recent years to redress the balance in favor of hotels in the mid- and low-priced categories, but it is a slow process. If a particular hotel strikes your fancy but is out of your price range, it may pay to inquire if special off-season, weekend, specific weekday, or other packages will bring prices down to what you can afford. Many hotels offer significant rate reductions between November 1 and March 31, except during the Christmas and New Year period.

Summer Stays: Reserve Ahead

July and August are tough months for finding hotel rooms in Amsterdam. Try to reserve as far ahead as possible for this period. If you have problems getting a room, contact the tourist information office, which can generally arrange a room somewhere though it might not be in the kind of hotel you are looking for and you might need to pay more for a room in a better-class hotel.

You can also reserve with the **Amsterdam Reservation Center** (☎ **020/201-8800;** fax 020/201-8850; reservations@atcb.nl; www. amsterdamtourist.nl).

reasonable price. The Smit's best feature is the Café Van Gogh on its ground floor, offering reasonably priced homemade meals in a trendy setting. Breakfast here (not included in room rates) features delicious Gouda omelets, Dutch pancakes, and fresh croissants. *Pieter Cornelisz Hooftstraat 24–28. ☎ 020/671-4785. www.hotelsmit.com. 106 units. Doubles 104€–135€. MC, V. Tram: 2 or 5 to Hobbemastraat. Map p 123.*

★ Vondelpark Museum B&B

MUSEUM DISTRICT   The affable Fontijn family owns this 1879 mansion overlooking Vondelpark. They rent out three apartments that sleep up to four people, and one charming double bedroom on the ground floor. All units come fully equipped with antique furniture and large windows with park views; the top-floor apartment has its own private rooftop terrace. There's no elevator. *Vossiusstraat 14. ☎ 020/676-2511. 4 units. Doubles 85€–95€ w/breakfast; apt 110€ without breakfast. No credit cards. Tram: 2 or 5 to Hobbemastraat. Map p 123.*

Winston OLD CENTER   Young partygoers flock to this vibrant budget hotel with two bars and a nightclub on the premises. It's on Amsterdam's oldest (and a somewhat seedy) street, mere steps from the Red Light District. Families may want to look elsewhere, but it's a great choice for hedonists. *Warmoesstraat 129. ☎ 020/623-1380. www.winston.nl. 69 units, 25 with bathroom. Doubles with bathroom 110€; doubles without bathroom 85€; all w/breakfast. AE, DC, MC, V. Tram: 4, 9, 14, 16, 24, or 25 to the Dam. Map p 124.* ●

The Vondelpark Museum B&B offers park views at bargain prices.

Haarlem

- **Canal boat cruises**
- ✝ **Church**
- ⓘ **Information**
- **Railway**

① Grote Markt
② Sint-Bavokerk
③ Dijkers
④ Woltheus Cruises
⑤ Teylers Museum
⑥ Frans Hals Museum

Previous page: Haarlem's picturesque town gate.

aarlem, a handsome town of 150,000 inhabitants, is where Rembrandt contemporaries Frans Hals, Jacob van Ruisdael, and Pieter Saenredam lived and painted their famous portraits, landscapes, and church interiors. Haarlem boasts one of the country's best museums and finest churches, but it has something of a traditional Dutch village feel that's typified by the lively open-air market on the main square. If you're traveling with kids, be sure to take a canal-boat cruise. START: **A 10-minute stroll south from Haarlem's Art Nouveau railway station, by way of Kruisweg, Kruisstraat, and Smedenstraat, brings you to the historic central market square.**

1 ★★★ **Grote Markt.** The monumental buildings around the tree-lined square, which date from the 15th to 19th centuries, are a visual minicourse in the development of Dutch architecture. The oldest building is Haarlem's 14th-century Stadhuis (Town Hall), a former hunting lodge that was rebuilt in the 17th century. *Market open Mon 8:30am–5pm; Sat 9am–5pm.*

2 ★★ **Sint-Bavokerk (St. Bavo's Church).** Completed in 1520, this magnificent church—also known as the Grote Kerk (Great Church)—has a rare unity of structure and proportion. Its elegant wooden tower is covered with lead sheets and adorned with gilt spheres. The light and airy church interior has whitewashed walls and

St. Bavo's famed Christian Müller organ.

sandstone pillars. But the most fascinating feature is the soaring Christian Müller organ (1738). It has 5,068 pipes and is nearly 30m (98 ft.) tall.

Grote Markt.

Haarlem Basics

For many Amsterdammers, Haarlem is not only the closest charming town for an afternoon of shopping at the market, but it's also home. Commuters crowd the trains to Haarlem in the early evening, but during the day the twice-hourly trains are close to empty (except on hot sunny days). The ride from Amsterdam's Centraal Station takes just 15 minutes, and the round-trip fare is 6.40€. Once in Haarlem, you can pretty much walk everywhere. Haarlem's Centraal Station is just a 10-minute walk from the market square and most of the attractions listed here.

For information, **VVV Haarlem,** Stationsplein 1, 2011 LR Haarlem (☎ **0900/616-1600;** fax 023/534-0537; www.vvvzk.nl), is just outside the rail station. The office is open October to March, Monday to Friday from 9:30am to 5:30pm and Saturday from 10am to 2pm; April to September, Monday to Friday from 9:30am to 5:30pm and Saturday from 10am to 4pm.

Mozart played the organ in 1766 when he was just 10 years old, and Handel and Liszt both made special visits here to play it. You can hear the organ in a free recital Tuesday at 8:15pm from May to October; in July and August there's an additional free recital on Thursday at 3pm. From May to October, church services using the organ take place Sunday at 10am; June to October there's an additional 7pm Vespers and Cantata service. 🕐 *45 min.*

Oude Groenmarkt 23. ☎ *023/553-2040. Admission 2€ adults, 1.25€ kids 12–16. Mon–Sat 10am–4pm.*

3 ★ Dijkers. This tiny restaurant, popular with locals, serves hearty lunches like Thai green curry and lighter fare such as club and toasted sandwiches. The mozarella and prosciutto is excellent. *Warmoesstraat 5–7.* ☎ *023/551-1564. $.*

A collection of fossils and minerals at the Teylers Museum.

Frans Hals's A Banquet of the Officers of the St. George Militia.

❹ ★ kids Post Verkade Cruises.
A canal cruise is an ideal way to get to know Haarlem. The dock is on the Spaarne River beside the Gravenstenenbrug, a handsome lift bridge. You'll see loads of historical buildings, and pass close to an 18th-century traditional Dutch windmill—a great photo op. ⏱ *1½ hr. At the Spaarne River and the Gravenstenenbrug.* ☎ *023/535-7723. www.post verkadecruises.nl. Tickets 9.50€ adults, 4.50€ kids 3–12. Apr–Oct Tues–Sun boats depart at noon, 1, 2, 3, and 4pm.*

❺ kids Teylers Museum. This quirky but interesting museum was the first museum to open in the Netherlands, in 1784. It's named after the 18th-century merchant Pieter Teyler van der Hulst, who willed his entire fortune for the advancement of both art and science. You'll find a diverse collection here: drawings by Michelangelo, Raphael, and Rembrandt (which are shown in rotation); fossils, minerals, and skeletons; and instruments of physics and an odd assortment of inventions, including the largest electrostatic generator in the world (built in 1784) and a 19th-century radarscope. ⏱ *1½ hr. Spaarne 16.*

☎ *023/531-9010. www.teylers museum.nl. 7€ adults; 3€ kids 6–17. Tues–Sat 10am–5pm; Sun and holidays noon–5pm. Closed Jan 1, Dec 25.*

❻ ★★★ Frans Hals Museum.
This superb museum is the highlight of many Dutch art lovers' trips to Holland. The 1608 building was once a majestic home for retired gentlemen. Consequently, the famous paintings by Frans Hals (1580–1686) and other masters of the Haarlem School hang in settings that look like the 17th-century houses they were intended to adorn. Hals earned his living by painting portraits of members of the local Schutters (Musketeers) Guild. Typified by his *A Banquet of the Officers of the St. George Civic Guard* (1616), five such works, with a style that inspired van Gogh, hang in the museum, along with six more paintings by Hals. Among other pieces is a superb dollhouse from around 1750, and fine collections of antique, silver, porcelain, and clocks. ⏱ *2 hr. Groot Heiligland 62.* ☎ *023/511-5775. www.franshals museum.com. Admission 7.50€ adults, 3.75€ ages 19–24. Tues–Sat 11am–5pm; Sun and holidays noon–5pm. Closed Jan 1 & Dec 25.*

The Hague & Scheveningen

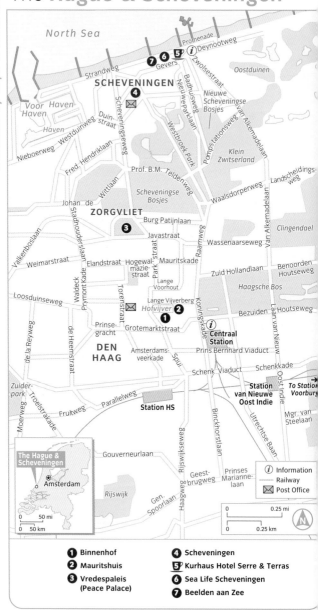

1 Binnenhof

2 Mauritshuis

3 Vredespaleis
(Peace Palace)

4 Scheveningen

5 Kurhaus Hotel Serre & Terras

6 Sea Life Scheveningen

7 Beelden aan Zee

The capital of the Netherlands is stately and grand, and its neighboring seacoast resort Scheveningen provides a lovely escape. A day here affords you a fantastic opportunity to visit the Peace Palace, home to the International Court of Justice, and the Binnenhof, the grand seat of the Dutch Parliament. The Hague (known in Dutch as Den Haag, or more formally as 's-Gravenhage) is only an hour away from Amsterdam, but you may consider spending a night here to have some beach time. START: **A 10-minute tram ride from Den Haag Centraal Station brings you to the center city at Buitenhof, the Outer Court of Holland's Parliament.**

❶ ★★★ Binnenhof (Inner Court). At this venerable complex of Parliament buildings, join a tour to visit the lofty, medieval Ridderzaal (Hall of the Knights), where the queen delivers a speech from the throne each year to open the new legislative session. Depending on the volume and urgency of government business, you may be able to tour one or the other of the two chambers of the Staaten-Generaal (States General), the Dutch Parliament. ⏱ *2 hr. Binnenhof 8A.* ☎ *070/ 364-6144. www.binnenhofbezoek.nl. Admission 8€ or 6€ adults (varies with the tour being offered), 1€ kids under 13. Guided tours (the only way you can visit) are given hourly Mon–Sat 10am–4pm. Be sure to call ahead to reserve a tour and to confirm availability. Occasionally tours are canceled because of government*

Maurtishuis at night.

Vermeer's famous Girl with a Pearl Earring.

business. During school holidays the tours fill up quickly and you may have to wait several hours if you don't have a booking. Tram: 10, 16, or 17 to Buitenhof.

❷ ★★★ Mauritshuis. Adjacent to the Binnenhof complex is this elegant Italian Renaissance–style museum. The villa was built in 1644 as the home of Count Johan Maurits van Nassau, a young court dandy and cousin of the Oranje-Nassaus. Today this small palace houses the Koninklijk Kabinet van Schilderijen (Royal Cabinet of Paintings) and is the permanent home of an impressive art collection given to the Dutch nation by King Willem I in 1816. Highlights include 13 Rembrandts, 3 Frans Hals's, and 3 Vermeers (including his famous *View of Delft* and *Girl with a Pearl Earring*). The museum's three floors are packed with hundreds of other works by

The Peace Palace.

such painters as Bruegel, Rubens, Steen, and Holbein (including his portrait of Jane Seymour, third wife of Henry VIII of England). If you love the Old Masters, this museum will take your breath away. ⏲ *2 hr. Korte Vijverberg 8.* ☎ *070/302-3435. www.mauritshuis.nl. Admission 9.50€ adults, free for kids under 19. Tues–Sat 10am–5pm (also Mon Apr–Oct); Sun and holidays 11am–5pm. Tram: 10, 16, or 17 to Buitenhof. Closed Jan 1 & Dec 25.*

❸ ★ **Vredespaleis (Peace Palace).** You'll have to call ahead for a tour reservation, but this could easily be the highlight of your trip to The Hague. Andrew Carnegie donated over a million dollars to the construction of this magnificent mock-Gothic Palace, home to the Permanent Court of Arbitration and the International Court of Justice. The building was designed by French architect Louis Cordonnier and completed in 1913. On the tour you'll be able to visit most of the rooms and marvel at gifts given by each of the participating countries: crystal chandeliers (each weighing 1,750kg/3,858 lb.) from Delft, made with real rubies and emeralds; incredible mosaic floors from France; 140 kinds of different marble from Italy; a huge Turkish carpet woven in 1926 in Izmir; and an immense 3,500kg (7,716-lb.) vase from Czar Nicolas of Russia. If the courts are not in session, your guide will take you inside the International Court of Justice, which handles all of the United Nations' judicial cases. ⏲ *2 hr. Carnegieplein 2.* ☎ *070/302-4137. www.vredespaleis.nl. Admission*

The Hague Basics

The Hague is an hour from Amsterdam's Centraal Station. Trains depart at least every half-hour. Note that the Dutch name for The Hague is the informal Den Haag, or the formal 's-Gravenhage. The one-way fare is 7.60€. Once you arrive at Den Haag Centraal Station, you'll find trams adjacent to the station. You can use any transit card purchased in Amsterdam here (indeed anywhere in the country). Otherwise, you'll pay 1.60€ or 2.40€ depending on your destination (or 1.20€ on tram no. 1 to Delft after 9am); the driver will sell you a ticket onboard. Tram no. 9 goes all the way to Scheveningen and back; in the opposite direction, it goes all the way to Delft. The ride from Scheveningen back to The Hague's Centraal Station takes 20 minutes.

For information, **VVV Den Haag,** Hofweg 1, 2500 CD Den Haag (☎ **0900/340-3505;** fax 070/347-2102; www.denhaag.com), is close to the Binnenhof (Parliament). The office is open Monday to Friday from 10am to 6pm, Saturday from 10am to 5pm, and Sunday from noon to 5pm.

5€ adults, free for kids under 13. Tours Mon–Fri 10 and 11am & 2, 3, and 4pm. Reservations required; it's not possible to visit the palace on your own. *Tram: 1 or 10 to Vredespaleis.*

④ ★★ Scheveningen. This relaxed, beachside town is only a 15-minute tram ride from the center of The Hague. It has a wide, sandy beach and a charming pier affording great views of the North Sea. Pleasant cafes line the waterfront boardwalk, and on summer weekends sun worshippers fill the beach. Towering over both the town and the beach is the majestic Kurhaus Hotel. Consider having a drink in the grand lobby or even a meal at one of the two restaurants, which have fine views of the water. If you're in the mood for some outdoor activity, you can take a long walk over the rolling sand dunes that dot the coast for miles. Turn right as you leave the hotel and in just 10 minutes you'll feel as if you're in the middle of nowhere. *Tram: 1, 9, or 11 to the beach; 10 or 17 to the fishing harbor.*

⑤ ★★★ Kurhaus Hotel Serre & Terras. I like to have a drink or a snack in the conservatory and terrace here while enjoying the views of the North Sea. If you're here on a cold afternoon, consider having the traditional English tea in the ultra-gracious lobby with its high ceiling and elaborate artwork. *Gevers Deynootplein 30.* ☎ *070/416-2636 Serre & Terras daily 10am–10pm; English tea Mon–Fri 3–6pm. $$$.*

⑥ ★★ kids Sea Life Scheveningen. This large aquarium has a walk-through underwater tunnel that lets you observe the denizens of the deep, including sharks swimming around above your head. *Strandweg (also known as the Boulevard) 13.* ☎ *070/354-2100. www.sealife.nl. Admission 12€ adults, 8.50€*

kids 3–11. Sept–June daily 10am–6pm; July–Aug daily 10am–8pm.

⑦ ★ Beelden aan Zee. A highlight of your trip to Scheveningen may be this fine sculpture museum built into the sand dunes just steps from the busy boardwalk and blending perfectly with the environment. Take some time to admire the construction and the use of natural light that spills into the main hall. Terraces overlooking the sea are strewn with sculptures and the indoor galleries look out onto the sand dunes and the sea beyond. Most of the sculptures are of human figures and the sculptors hail from all over the world. One of my favorites is the marble *Venus* (1984) by Dutch sculptor Jan Meefout. There are several temporary exhibits during the year, highlighting contemporary sculptors from around the world. Outside the museum, on the boardwalk, you'll find the Fairy Figures by the Sea, a permanent extension that's open free of charge. The huge, cartoonlike sculptures are all by New Yorker Tom Otterness. Leave some time to stroll around after you visit, admiring the sculptures from the pier and the beach. ⏱ *1½ hr. Hartevelstraat 1.* ☎ *070/358-5857. www.beeldenaan zee.nl. Admission 7€ adults, 3.50€ kids under 19. Tues–Sun 11am–5pm.*

Sharks cruise overhead at Sea Life Scheveningen.

Delft

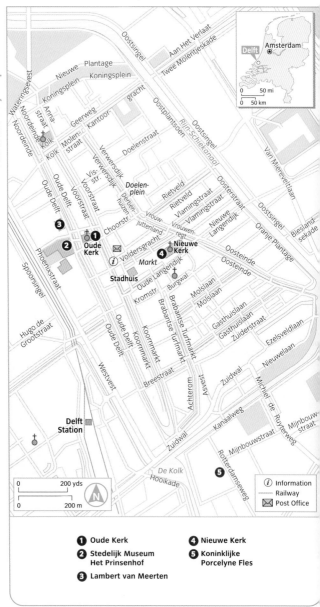

❶ Oude Kerk

❷ Stedelijk Museum
Het Prinsenhof

❸ Lambert van Meerten

❹ Nieuwe Kerk

❺ Koninklijke
Porcelyne Fles

Delft is best known as the home of the famous blue-and-white porcelain, and on this tour you'll visit the factory where it's produced. Delft is also a small, charming city that was the cradle of the Dutch Republic, the burial place of the royal family, and the birthplace and inspiration of artist Jan Vermeer, the 17th-century master of light and subtle emotion. Take a stroll through Delft and admire the colorful flower boxes and linden trees bending over gracious canals. START: **To reach the centrally located Oude Kerk from Delft's railway station, the most scenic walking route is along canalside Oude Delft, through the heart of the Old Town.**

① ★★ **Oude Kerk (Old Church).** Vermeer's house is long gone from Delft, as are his paintings, but he's buried at the Oude Kerk. This immense 13th-century church is notable for its 27 stained-glass windows. Also note the leaning clock tower built in the 14th century and the Gothic north transept, which was added in the 16th century by Belgian architect Anthonis Keldermans. The interior floors are paved with tomb slabs from the 17th century. *Heilige Geestkerkhof.* ☎ *015/212-3015. Admission (combined with Nieuwe Kerk; see below) 3.20€ adults, 1.60€*

A medieval gate.

ude Kerk, with its leaning clock tower.

kids 5–14. Apr–Oct Mon–Sat 9am–6pm; Nov–Mar Mon–Fri 11am–4pm, Sat 10am–5pm.

② ★★ **Stedelijk Museum Het Prinsenhof.** The "Father of the Nation," William I of Orange (William the Silent), lived and had his headquarters in this former convent during the years when he helped found the Dutch Republic. He was assassinated here, in 1584, and you can still see the musket-ball holes in the stairwell. Today the Prinsenhof is a museum of paintings, tapestries, silverware, and pottery. On the top floor, don't miss the accurately lit

Delft Basics

Delft is only 15 minutes by train (or 25 min. by tram) from The Hague. You'll have to change trains in The Hague to get here from Amsterdam, an easy feat, or you can combine a visit to Delft with a visit to The Hague or Rotterdam. The round-trip fare from Amsterdam is 21€. Or you can travel just to The Hague and then jump on a tram to Delft. From the Delft railway station, most everything is just a 10-minute walk. Tram no. 1 does the journey from The Hague to Delft two to three times an hour.

For information, **Tourist Information Delft,** Hippolytusbuurt 4, 2611 HN Delft (☎ **015/215-4051;** www.delft.nl), is in the center of town. The office is open April to September, Sunday and Monday from 10am to 6pm, Tuesday to Friday from 9am to 6pm, and Saturday from 10am to 5pm; October to March, Sunday from 11am to 4pm, and Tuesday to Saturday from 10am to 4pm.

and detailed features of every militiaman's face in Jan Michielsz van Mierevelt's *Civic Guard Banquet* (1611). There is also a beautiful collection of Dutch wineglasses from the 17th century. ⏲ *1 hr. Sint-Agathaplein 1.* ☎ *015/260-2358. www.prinsenhof-delft.nl. Admission 6€ adults, 5€ kids 12–16. Tues–Sat 10am–5pm; Sun and holidays 1–5pm. Closed Jan 1 & Dec 25.*

❸ ★ **Lambert van Meerten.** A visit to this elaborately designed canalside home will give you a glimpse into the lives of the prosperous in Delft. Built in 1892 for a wealthy patron of the arts, Lambert van Meerten, this beautiful neo-Renaissance-style house has a fine collection of antique blue-and-white Delft tiles displayed on the wood-paneled walls. Be sure to look up at the Delft vases placed discreetly above the doorframes. Even the fireplace is adorned with Delft tiles. After your visit it's worth a stroll across the canal to admire the house from afar. ⏲ *45 min. Best time to come is late afternoon, when it's less crowded and the sun slanting* *through the back windows splashes the tiles with light. Oude Delft 199.* ☎ *015/260-2358. www.gemeente musea-delft.nl. Admission 6€ adults, 5€ kids 12–16. Tues–Sat 10am–5pm; Sun and holidays 1–5pm. Closed Jan 1 & Dec 25.*

❹ ★ **Nieuwe Kerk.** Prince William of Orange and other members of the House of Oranje-Nassau are buried

The interior of the Nieuwe Kerk.

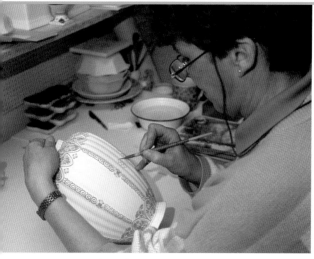

You can see artists at work at Delft's porcelain factory.

here. The church was built between 1383 and 1510, and most of it was restored following a fire in 1536. Renowned architect PJH Cuypers added the 100m (328-ft.) tower to the Gothic facade. Dutch architect and sculptor Hendrick de Keyser designed the ornate black-and-white marble tomb of William of Orange. After your visit to the interior, stroll around the square, admiring the church and its spire from different angles. *Markt.* ☎ *015/212-3025. Admission (combined with Oude Kerk; see above) 3.20€ adults, 1.60€ kids 5–14. Apr–Oct Mon–Sat 9am–6pm; Nov–Mar Mon–Fri 11am–4pm, Sat 11am–5pm.*

⑤ ★ Koninklijke Porcelyne Fles. If you like Delft porcelain, you'll be in heaven at the Royal Delft factory. Not only will you get to visit the factory and get a firsthand view of the business of painting porcelain, but you can also visit the Delft museum and shop at the showroom for factory seconds at incredible bargains. But perhaps the highlight of any visit here is the 2½-hour workshop that teaches you to paint your own porcelain, which is then fired and glazed and ready for pickup after 48 hours (or it can be shipped to your home address). The workshop cost includes the materials but not the shipping and handling costs. These workshops are available from 9am to 3pm, and it's advisable to call ahead for reservations. *Rotterdamseweg 196.* ☎ *015/ 251-2030. www.royaldelft.com. Tour 4€ adults, free for kids under 13; 1-hr. workshop 48€ adults, 23€ kids under 12. Mid-Mar to Oct daily 9am–5pm; Nov to mid-Mar Mon–Sat 9am–5pm. Closed Dec 25–Jan 1.*

Rotterdam

(i) Information
✉ Post Office

1 Spido Harbor Tour
2 Euromast
3 Hotel New York
4 Museum Boijmans Van Beuningen
5 Arboretum Trompenburg

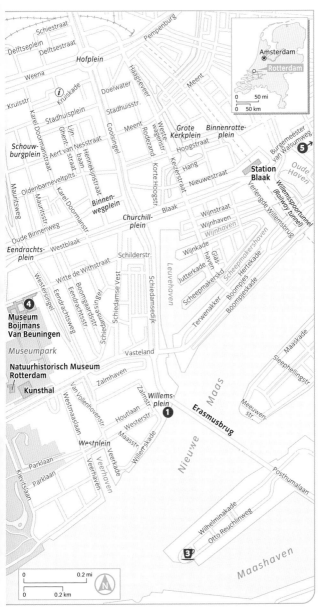

Schiestraat
Delftseplein
Delftsestraat
Hofplein
Weena
Pempenburg
Haagseveer
Doelwater
Meent
Amsterdam
Rotterdam
0   50 mi
0   50 km
Kruisstr.
(i) Kruiskade
Stadhuisplein
Stadhuisstr.
Karel Doormanstraat
Lijn-
baan
Ghent-
straat
Aert van Nesstraat
Henneklijnstraat
Karel Doormanstr
Meent
Weste-
wagenstr
Rodezand
Korte Hoogstr.
Grote
Kerkplein
Hoogstraat
Binnenrotte-
plein
Burgemeester
van Walsumweg
Schouw-
burgplein
Oldenbarneveltplts.
Binnen-
wegplein
Keizerstraat
Hang
Nieuwestraat
Station
Blaak
Oude
Haven
Mauritsweg
Mauritsstr.
Oude Binnenweg
Westblaak
Churchill-
plein
Blaak
Wijnstraat
Wijnhaven
Wijnhaven
Verlengde Willemsbrug
Willemsspoortunnel
(Railway tunnel)
Eendrachts-
plein
Westersingel
Witte de Withstraat
Boomgaardsstr.
Boomgaardsstr
Schiedamse Vest
Schilderstr.
Schiedamsedijk
Leuvehaven
Wijnkade
Jutterkade
Glas-
haven
Scheepmakershaven
Scheepmakersd
Scheepmakershaven
Hertekade
Boompjes
Boompjeskade
Boompjes
Terwenakker
Maaskade
Eendrachtsweg
Eendrachtsstr
Schiedamsedijk
Museum
Boijmans
Van Beuningen
Museumpark
Natuurhistorisch Museum
Rotterdam
Kunsthal
Vasteland
Sleephellingstr
Van Vollenhovenstr.
Zalmhaven
Houtlaan
Zalmstr.
Willems-
plein
Erasmusbrug
Maas
Meeuwen
str.
Westmaaslaan
Westerstr.
Maasstr.
Westplein
Willemskade
Maaskade
Parklaan
Veerkade
Veerhaven
Nieuwe
Parklaan
Klevitslaan
Posthumalaan
Wilhelminakade
Otto Reuchlinweg
Maashaven

0   0.2 mi
0   0.2 km

Affectionately referred to as "Manhattan on the Maas" (the river that runs through it and out to the North Sea), Rotterdam was almost entirely destroyed during World War II. Its vibrant newness is part of its attraction. Rotterdam also has an important place in American history: Delfshaven, one of the only areas not wrecked during World War II, is the port from which the Pilgrim Fathers sailed to the new continent. START: **Rotterdam is a spread-out, modern city, and most of it doesn't really reward a lot of walking. You're advised to go by Metro train to Leuvehaven, or by tram even closer, to the Spido tour-boat dock on the Maas.**

❶ ★ kids Spido Harbor Tour.
The best way to tour Rotterdam is by taking this large, comfortable boat up and down the Maas River and deep into the world's largest port. You pass under the city's most scenic landmark, the Erasmus Bridge (or Swan Bridge as it's been dubbed by the locals), and you pass Delfshaven and its old mill (from where the pilgrims left for America in 1620). You get fabulous views of the Euromast, Rotterdam's tallest structure, built in 1960. But the most fascinating aspect of this tour is its up-close-and-personal view of the workings of this immense port: You zigzag around giant cranes, tankers, barges, and all kinds of boats and ships. Older kids and anybody with a maritime interest will love this trip. ⏱ 1¼ hr. Willemsplein 85 (under the Erasmus Bridge).

Get an up-close look at the Erasmus Bridge on a tour of Rotterdam's harbor.

☎ 010/275-9988. www.spido.nl. Tickets 9.25€ adults, 5.80€ kids 4–11. Apr–Sept departures every

Delfshaven.

Rotterdam Basics

Trains leave Amsterdam's Centraal Station every half-hour for the 1-hour ride to Rotterdam. Some trains make a stop in The Hague before reaching Rotterdam, adding 5 minutes to the trip. The round-trip fare is 24€. Once in Rotterdam, you can use the trams with the same card you used in Amsterdam. Taxis are plentiful, too.

For information, **VVV Rotterdam Store,** Coolsingel 5, 3012 AA Rotterdam (☎ **0900/403-4065;** fax 010/271-0128; www.vvvrotterdam. nl; Metro: Stadhuis), is on the corner of Hofplein. The office is open Monday to Thursday and Saturday from 9am to 5pm, Friday from 9am to 9pm, and Sunday from 10am to 5pm.

30–45 min. 9:30am–5pm; Oct–Mar usually 2–3 trips per day with the last one at 3pm; check the website or call ahead for winter hours. Tram: 7 to Willemsplein.

2 ★★ **Euromast.** This slender tower, 185m (607 ft.) tall, is indisputably the best vantage point for an overall view of Rotterdam and its environs, out to 30km (19 miles) on a clear day. You can have lunch or dinner in the Euromast Brasserie, 100m (328 ft.) above the harbor park, while enjoying spectacular views of the port. A rotating elevator departs from here for the Euroscoop viewing platform. From the Brasserie level, for an additional payment, you can abseil or rope slide back to the ground—definitely not for the faint of heart. *Parkhaven 20.* ☎ *010/436-4811. www.euromast. nl. Admission 8.30€ adults, 5.40€ kids 4–11. Apr–Sept daily 9:30am–11pm; Oct–Mar daily 10am–11pm. Tram: 8 to Euromast.*

3 **Hotel New York.** What was once the headquarters for the Holland America shipping lines is now a modern hotel with a lovely cafe-restaurant on its ground floor. You can take a water taxi to get here

(from the tiny marina at the edge of Veerkade facing the Wereldmuseum). The water taxi, small and wooden, is in itself part of the Hotel New York's allure. It costs 2.70€ each way. Once here, settle into a waterside table and enjoy large American-style salads (like Chef's or Caesar) or order some samples from the wonderful oyster bar. If there are strong winds, the water taxi will not operate and you can just hail a normal cab that will drive you to the left bank over the Erasmus bridge (a 5-min. trip); or board tram no. 20, 23, or 25 from the nearby Leuvehaven stop. *Koninginnenhoofd 1.* ☎ *010/439-0500. www. hotelnewyork.nl. $$.*

4 ★★ **Museum Boijmans Van Beuningen.** Hail a cab or take the tram to yet another of Holland's treasure troves of fine art. Here, you'll find walls and walls of paintings by the Dutch masters as well as works by Degas, Dali, Man Ray, and Tintoretto. There's a fine collection of porcelain, silver, glass, and delftware, too. Don't miss Rembrandt's moving *Titus at his Desk* (1655), which depicts his son deep in thought with the gentlest play of light and shadow to portray a

A Grand Harbor

A dredged deep-water channel connects Rotterdam with the North Sea and forms a 40km-long (25-mile) harbor. The Port of Rotterdam is the world's second or third busiest port (after Shanghai and about equal with Singapore)—handling 37,000 ships and 410 million metric tons of cargo. You may think visiting a harbor is boring business on a vacation, but Rotterdam's is one of the most memorable sights in Holland and likely makes any other harbor you've ever seen look like a Fisher-Price toy.

Container ships, bulk carriers, tankers, and careworn tramps are waited on by a vast retinue of machines and people. Trucks, trains, and barges, each carrying its little piece of the action, hurry into and out from the hub. Rotterdam is the pump that replenishes Europe's commercial arteries.

slightly brooding mood. Among the many distinguished objects from the 17th century is a walnut-wood clock 2m (7 ft.) tall that will take your breath away. When you're done, you can take a 15-minute walk back to the railway station or catch the tram or a taxi. *Museumpark 18–20.* ☎ *010/441-9400. www.boijmans.rotterdam.nl. Admission 9€ adults, free for kids under 19. Tues–Sun 11am–5pm. Closed Jan 1, Apr 30 & Dec 25. Tram: 7 to Eendrachtsplein.*

⑤ ★ Arboretum Trompenburg. East of the center city, this city jewel has evolved from a family-owned 19th-century estate into a gorgeous garden kept in good order by an army of gardeners. Trompenburg contains more than 4,000 trees, bushes, and perennials, with oak, pine, cedar, ash, yew, hostas, and rhododendron among those on the roster. In addition, the arboretum has a rose garden, a goldfish pond, an aviary, and a hothouse full of cacti and succulents. *Honingerdijk 86 (close to Erasmus University).* ☎ *010/233-0166. www.trompenburg.nl. Admission 4€ adults, free for accompanied*

kids under 13. Mon–Fri 9am–5pm; Sat–Sun 10am–4pm (Sun noon–4pm Nov–Mar). Closed Dec 23–Jan 7 (the closed dates might vary by a few days). Tram: 7 or 21 to Woudestein. ●

Hotel New York.

The **Savvy Traveler**

Centraal Station

Before You Go

Government Tourist Offices

For the U.S. & Canada: Netherlands Board of Tourism & Conventions (NBTC), 355 Lexington Ave., 19th Floor, New York, NY 10017 (☎ 212/370-7360; fax 212/370-9507; www.holland.com). **For the U.K. & Ireland:** No walk-in service. NBTC, PO Box 30783, London WC2B 6DH (☎ 020/7539-7950; fax 020/7539-7953; www.holland.com/uk). **In Holland:** No walk-in service. NBTC, Postbus 458, 2260 MG Leidschendam (☎ 31-70/370-5705; fax 31-70/320-1654; info@holland.com; www.holland.com).

The Best Times to Go

"In season" in Amsterdam means from mid-April to mid-October. The peak of the tourist season is July and August, when the weather is at its finest. Weather, however, is never really extreme at any time of year, and if you're one of the growing numbers who favor shoulder- or off-season travel, you'll find the city every bit as attractive. Not only are airlines, hotels, and restaurants cheaper and less crowded during the off season (with more relaxed and personalized service), but there are also some very appealing events going on. You may want to go when the bulb fields near Amsterdam are bursting with color from April to mid-May, one of the best times to visit Holland.

Festivals & Special Events

SPRING. Late March to mid-May, catch the **Opening of Keukenhof Gardens,** Lisse. The greatest flower show on Earth blooms with a spectacular display of tulips, narcissi, daffodils, hyacinths, bluebells, crocuses, lilies, amaryllis, and many other flowers at this 32-hectare (79-acre) garden in the heart of the bulb country. There's said to be nearly eight million flowers, but who's counting? Contact **Keukenhof** (☎ 0252/465-555; www.keukenhof.nl).

During **National Museum Weekend** (the second weekend in Apr), most museums in Amsterdam and many throughout the Netherlands offer free or reduced admission and have special exhibits.

On April 30 Amsterdam celebrates **Koninginnedag (Queen's Day)** with a gigantic dawn-to-dawn street carnival. The center city gets so jampacked with people that it's virtually impossible to move. A citywide street market features masses of stalls. Orange ribbons, orange hair, and orange-painted faces are everywhere, as are Dutch flags. Street music and theater combine with lots of drinking during this good-natured if boisterous affair. *Tip:* Wear something orange, even if it's only an orange cap or an orange ribbon in your hair. Contact **VVV Amsterdam** (☎ 0900/400-4040; www.amsterdamtourist.nl) for more information.

The second Saturday in May is **National Windmill Day** throughout Holland. Around two-thirds of the country's almost 1,000 remaining working windmills spin their sails and are open to the public; among them are Amsterdam's eight. Contact **De Hollandsche Molen** (☎ 020/623-8703; www.molens.nl).

SUMMER. From June to mid-August, catch a performance at the **Vondelpark Open-Air Theater.** Everything goes here: theater, all kinds of music (including full-scale classical concerts by the famed Royal Concertgebouw Orchestra), dance, and even

Previous page: Centraal Station.

operettas. Contact Vondelpark Openluchttheater (☎ 020/428-3360; www.openluchttheater.nl).

The **Amsterdam Roots Festival,** which runs for more than a week mid-June at various venues around town, features world music and dance, along with workshops, films, and exhibits. One part is the open-air **Oosterpark Festival,** a multicultural feast of song and dance held at Oosterpark in Amsterdam-Oost (East). Contact **Amsterdam Roots Festival** (☎ 020/531-8181; www.amsterdamroots.nl).

In the third week of June, **Open Garden Days** is your chance to find out what the fancy gardens behind the gables of some of the city's houses-turned-museums look like. A number of the best gardens are open to the public for 3 days. Go to the website of **Grachten Musea** (www.grachtenmusea.nl) for more information.

One of the world's leading gatherings of top international jazz and blues musicians, the **North Sea Jazz Festival** unfolds over 3 concert-packed mid-July days at Rotterdam's giant Ahoy! venue. Last-minute tickets are scarce, so book as far ahead as possible. Contact **North Sea Jazz Festival** (☎ 0900/300-1250 in Holland; 31-10/591-9000 from outside Holland; www.northseajazz.com).

Europe's most gay-friendly city hosts the **Amsterdam Gay Pride** event over 3 days in early August. A crowd of 150,000 people turns out to watch the Boat Parade, in which some 100 outrageously decorated boats cruise the canals. In addition, there are street discos, open-air theater performances, a sports program, and a film festival. Go to the website of **Amsterdam Gay Pride** (www.amsterdamgaypride.nl) for more information.

The 9-day classical music **Grachten Festival** plays in mid-August at various intimate and elegant venues along the canals and at the Muiziekgebouw aan 't IJ. Part of the festival is the exuberant Prinsengracht Concert, which is presented on a pontoon in front of the Hotel Pulitzer (p 132). Contact **Stichting Grachtenfestival** (☎ 020/421-4542; www.grachtenfestival.nl) for more information.

Amsterdam previews its soon-to-open cultural season with the **Uitmarkt,** usually the last weekend in August. A 3-day "open information market" runs alongside free performances of music, opera, dance, theater, and cabaret at theaters, concert halls, and impromptu outdoor venues around the city. Go to the website of **Uitmarkt** (www.uitmarkt.nl) for more information.

FALL. During **Open Monumentendag,** on the second Saturday in September, you have a chance to see historical buildings and monuments that are usually not open to the public—and to get in free as well. Contact **Vereniging Open Monumentendag** (☎ 020/422-2118; www.openmonumentendag.nl) for more information.

On the third Sunday in September, starting at noon, participants in the popular **Dam to Damloop (Dam to Dam Run),** start at the Dam in the center of Amsterdam, head out of town through the IJ Tunnel to the center of Zaandam, and return to the Dam, for a distance of 16km (10 miles). Contact **Dam to Damloop** (☎ 072/533-8136; www.damloop.nl) for more information.

On the third Tuesday in September, Queen Beatrix rides in a splendid gold coach to the Ridderzaal (Hall of the Knights) in The Hague for the **State Opening of Parliament,** which opens the legislative session.

Contact **VVV Den Haag** (☎ 0900/340-5051; www.denhaag.com) for more information.

Sinterklaas, Holland's equivalent of Santa Claus (St. Nicholas) launches the Christmas season on the third Saturday of November, when he arrives in the city by boat at the Centraal Station pier. Accompanied by black-painted assistants called *Zwarte Piet* (Black Peter) who hand out candy to kids along the way, he goes in stately procession through Amsterdam before being given the keys to the city by the mayor at the Dam. Contact **VVV Amsterdam** (☎ 0900/400-4040; www.amsterdamtourist.nl) for more information.

WINTER. The city's **New Year's** celebrations take place throughout the center city on the night of December 31 to January 1, but mostly at the Dam and Nieuwmarkt. Things can get wild and not always so wonderful. Many of Amsterdam's youthful spirits celebrate the new year with firecrackers, which they throw at the feet of passersby. This keeps hospital emergency departments busy.

More than 300 indie films are screened at theaters around town during the **Rotterdam International Film Festival,** from late January to early February. Contact (☎ 010/890-9090; www.filmfestivalrotterdam.com) for more information.

The Weather

Summers are warm and pleasant, with only a few oppressively hot days. However, air-conditioned hotels are rare, so those few days can be quite uncomfortable. Rain is common throughout the year, especially in winter.

Useful Websites

- www.visitholland.com offers comprehensive information, covering hotels, sightseeing, and notices of special events.

- www.amsterdamhotspots.nl lists the latest places to see and be seen in the city.

- www.hollandmuseums.nl is loaded with information about the city's museums—more than 40 of them.

Cell (Mobile) Phones

If your phone has GSM (Global System for Mobiles) capability and you have a world-compatible phone, you should be able to make and receive calls in Holland. Only certain phones have this capability, though, and you should check with your service operator first. Call charges can be high. Alternatively, you can rent a phone through **Cellhire** (www.cellhire.com; www.cellhire.co.uk; www.cellhire.com.au). After a simple online registration, they will ship a phone (usually with a U.K. number) to your home or office. Usage charges can be astronomical, so read the fine print.

U.K. mobiles work in Holland; call your service provider before departing your home country to ensure that the international call bar has been switched off and to check call charges, which can be extremely high. Also remember that you are

AMSTERDAM'S AVERAGE MONTHLY TEMPERATURES												
	JAN	FEB	MAR	APR	MAY	JUNE	JULY	AUG	SEPT	OCT	NOV	DEC
Temp. (°F)	36	36	41	46	54	59	62	62	58	51	44	38
Temp. (°C)	2	2	5	8	12	15	17	17	14	11	7	3

charged for calls you *receive* on a U.K. mobile used abroad.

Car Rentals

There's very little need to rent a car in Amsterdam, but if you're determined to do so, it's usually cheapest to book a car online before you leave home. Try **Hertz** (www.hertz.com), **Avis** (www.avis.com), or **Budget** (www.budget.com). You should also consider **AutoEurope** (www.auto europe.com), which sends you a prepaid voucher, locking in the exchange rate.

Getting **There**

By Plane

Arriving: Amsterdam Airport Schiphol (0900/0141 for general and flight information; 31-20/794-0800 from outside Holland; www.schiphol.nl), 13km (8 miles) southwest of the city center, is the main airport in the Netherlands, handling just about all of the country's international arrivals and departures. Frequent travelers regularly vote Schiphol (pronounced *Skhip*-ol) one of the world's favorite airports for its ease of use and its massive, duty-free shopping center.

After you deplane at one of the three terminals (all close together and numbered 1, 2, and 3), moving walkways take you to the Arrivals Hall, where you pass through Passport Control, Customs, and Baggage Reclaim. Conveniences like free luggage carts, currency exchange, ATMs, restaurants, bars, shops, baby rooms, restrooms, and showers are available. Beyond these is Schiphol Plaza, which combines rail station access, the Airport Hotel, a mall (sporting that most essential Dutch service—a flower store), bars and restaurants, restrooms, baggage lockers, airport and tourist information desks, car-rental and hotel-reservation desks, and more, all in a single location. Bus and shuttle stops and a taxi stand are just outside.

For tourist information and to make hotel reservations, go to the **Holland Tourist Information** desk in Schiphol Plaza (0900/400-4040); it is open daily from 7am to 10pm.

Getting into town: Netherlands Railways (NS) **trains** (0900/9292; www.ns.nl) for Amsterdam Centraal Station depart from Schiphol Station, downstairs from Schiphol Plaza, and stop at De Lelylaan and De Vlugtlaan stations in west Amsterdam on the way. Frequency ranges from six trains an hour at peak times to one an hour at night. The fare is 3.80€ one-way; the ride takes 15 to 20 minutes.

An alternative rail route serves both Amsterdam Zuid/WTC (World Trade Center) station and RAI station (beside the big RAI Convention Center). If you're staying at a hotel near Leidseplein, Rembrandtplein, in the Museum District, or in Amsterdam South, this route may be a better bet for you than Centraal Station. The fare is 3,80€ one-way; the ride takes around 15 minutes. From Amsterdam Zuid/WTC, take tram no. 5 for Leidseplein and the Museum District; from RAI, take tram no. 4 for Rembrandtplein.

The **Connexxion Schiphol Hotel Shuttle** (0900/9292; www.connexxion.nl) runs between the airport and Amsterdam, serving around 100 hotels either directly or because they are close to the direct stops. The fare is 12€ one-way and 19€ round-trip.

No reservations are needed and buses depart from in front of Schiphol Plaza every 10 to 30 minutes daily from 6am to 9pm. The bus ride takes anywhere from 40 minutes to 1½ hours.

The **Connexxion Interliner bus no. 370** departs every half-hour from in front of Schiphol Plaza for Amsterdam's downtown Marnixstraat bus station. The fare is 3.60€. The bus ride takes about 30 minutes.

You'll find **taxis** waiting at the stand of **SchipholTaxi** (☎ 0900/900-6666; www.schipholtaxi.nl) in front of Schiphol Plaza. Taxis from the airport are metered. Expect to pay around 40€ to the center city; the taxi ride to the center of Amsterdam takes 35 to 45 minutes. A service charge is already included in the fare.

By Boat from Britain
DFDS Seaways (☎ 0871/522-9955 in Britain; 0255/546-688 in Holland; www.dfdsseaways.co.uk) has daily car-ferry service between Newcastle in northeast England and IJmuiden on the North Sea coast west of Amsterdam. The overnight travel time is 15 hours. From IJmuiden, you can go by special bus to Amsterdam Centraal Station.

P&O Ferries (☎ 08701/664-5645 Britain; 020/200-8333 Holland; www.poferries.com) has daily car-ferry service between Hull in northeast England and Rotterdam (Europoort). The overnight travel time is 10 hours. Ferry-company buses shuttle passengers between the Rotterdam Europoort terminal and Rotterdam Centraal Station, from where there are frequent trains to Amsterdam.

Stena Line (☎ 08705/707070 in Britain; 0900/8123 in Holland; www.stenaline.co.uk) has twice-daily car-ferry service between Harwich in southeast England and Hoek van Holland (Hook of Holland) near

Rotterdam. The travel time is 6 hours, 15 minutes for the daytime crossing, and 7 hours for the overnight. Frequent trains depart from Hoek van Holland to Amsterdam.

By Cruise Ship
Cruise-ship passengers arrive in Amsterdam at the **Passenger Terminal Amsterdam,** Piet Heinkade 27 (☎ 020/509-1000; www.pt amsterdam.nl; tram: 25 or 26), on the IJ waterway within easy walking distance of Centraal Station.

By Train
Rail service to Amsterdam from other cities in the Netherlands and elsewhere in Europe is frequent and fast. International trains arrive at Centraal Station from Brussels, Paris, Berlin, Cologne and other German cities, and from more cities in Austria, Switzerland, Italy, and eastern Europe. **Nederlandse Spoorwegen** (Netherlands Railways; www.ns.nl) trains arrive in Amsterdam from towns and cities all over Holland. Service is frequent to many places around the country and trains are modern, clean, and punctual. Schedule and fare information on travel by train and other public transportation (openbaar vervoer) in the Netherlands is available by calling ☎ 0900/9292, or visiting www.9292ov.nl; for international trains, call ☎ 0900/9296.

The burgundy-colored **Thalys** (www.thalys.com) high-speed train, with a top speed of 300kmph (186 mph), connects Paris, Brussels, Amsterdam, and (via Brussels) Cologne. Travel time from Paris to Amsterdam is 4 hours and 10 minutes, and from Brussels 2 hours and 45 minutes. For Thalys information and reservations, call ☎ 03635 in France; ☎ 02/528-2828 in Belgium; ☎ 11861 in Germany; and ☎ 0900/9296 in Holland. Tickets are also available from many railway stations and travel agents.

On the **Eurostar** (www.eurostar. com) high-speed train (top speed 300kmph/186 mph), the travel time between London Waterloo Station and Brussels Midi Station (the closest connecting point for Amsterdam) is around 2 hours. Departures from London to Brussels are approximately every 2 hours at peak times. For Eurostar reservations, call ☎ 08705/186186 in Britain.

Arriving at Centraal Station: Regardless of where they originate, most visitors traveling to Amsterdam by train find themselves deposited at Amsterdam's Centraal Station, built from 1884 to 1889 on an artificial island in the IJ channel. The building, an ornate architectural wonder on its own, is the focus of much activity. It's at the hub of the city's concentric rings of canals and connecting main streets, and is the originating point for most of the city's trams, Metro trains, and buses.

You'll find an office of VVV Amsterdam tourist information inside the station on platform 2 and another office right in front of the station on Stationsplein; both offices have hotel-reservation desks. Other facilities include a GWK Travelex currency-exchange office, ATMs, a train info center, luggage lockers, restaurants and snack bars, newsstands, and some small specialty stores.

Warning: Centraal Station is home to a pickpocket convention that's in full swing at all times. Messages broadcast in multiple languages warn people to be on their guard, but the artful dodgers still seem to do good business. Avoid becoming one of their victims by keeping your money and other valuables under wraps, especially among crowds. You're also likely to notice a heroin addict or two, a platoon of panhandlers, and more than a whiff of pot smoke on the air.

An array of tram stops are on either side of the main station exit—virtually all of Amsterdam's hotels are within a 15-minute tram ride from Centraal Station. The Metro station is downstairs, just outside the main exit. City bus stops are to the left of the main exit, and the taxi stands are to the right. At the public transportation GVB Tickets & Info office on Stationsplein, you can buy cards for trams, Metro trains, and buses (see "Getting Around," below, for more information). The station is also a departure point for passenger ferries across the IJ waterway, water taxis, canal-boat tours, the Museumboat, and the Canal Bus.

By Bus

International coaches—and in particular those of **Eurolines** (www. eurolines.com)—arrive at the bus terminal opposite the Amstel rail station (Metro: Amstel) in the south of the city. **Eurolines** operates coach service between London Victoria Bus Station and Amstel Station (via ferry), with up to five departures daily in the summer. Travel time is just over 12 hours. For reservations, contact Eurolines (☎ 08717/818181 in Britain or 020/560-8788 in Holland). From here you can go by train or Metro train to Centraal Station, or by tram no. 12 to the Museumplein area and to connecting points for trams to the center city. For the Leidseplein area, take the Metro toward Centraal Station, get out at Weesperplein, and go aboveground to take tram line 7 or 10.

By Car

A network of major international highways crisscrosses Holland. European expressways E19, E35, E231, and E22 converge on Amsterdam from France and Belgium to the south and from Germany to the north and east. These roads also have Dutch designations; as you approach the city they are, respectively: A4, A2, A1, and A7. Amsterdam's ring road is A10. Distances between destinations are relatively short. Traffic is invariably heavy, but road conditions are otherwise excellent, service stations are plentiful, and highways are plainly signposted.

Getting **Around**

By Public Transportation

By 2009, all public transportation in the Netherlands should be using an electronic stored-value card called the **OV-chipkaart** in place of the old tickets. There are three main types of OV-chipkaart: "personal" cards that can be used only by their pictured owner; "anonymous" cards that can be used by anyone; and "throwaway" cards. The personal and anonymous cards, both valid for 5 years, cost 7.50€ and can be loaded and reloaded with up to 30€. Throwaway cards, which are likely to be the card of choice for short-term visitors, cost 2.50€ for one ride and 4.80€ for two rides. Reduced-rate cards are available for seniors and children. Electronic readers on Metro and train station platforms and onboard trams and buses deduct the correct fare; just hold your card up against the reader at both the start and the end of the ride. **Remember:** These cards are valid not just in Amsterdam, but also everywhere in Holland, no matter where you buy them or use them.

Visitors intending to make frequent use of all of Amsterdam's public transportation options might consider purchasing the **All Amsterdam Transport Pass,** valid on the Canal Bus, trams, buses, and the Metro. It costs 24€ a day and is available from the GVB Tickets & Info office, VVV tourist information offices, and the Canal Bus company. It's a good value if you make extensive use of its unlimited travel facility on both the Canal Bus and GVB public transportation.

By Tram: Half the fun of Amsterdam is walking along the canals. The other half is riding the blue-and-light-gray trams that roll through most major streets. There are 16 tram routes, 10 of which (lines 1, 2, 4, 5, 9, 13, 16, 17, 24, and 26) begin and end at Centraal Station; another (line 25) passes through. So you know you can always get back to that central point if you get lost and have to start over. The city's other tram lines are 3, 7, 10, 12, and 14.

Most trams have just one available access door that opens automatically; you board toward the rear (in the case of the oldest trams, at the rear) following arrowed indicators that point the way to the door. To board a tram that has no such arrowed indicators, push the button on the outside of the car beside any door. To get off, you may need to push a button with an "open-door" graphic or the words *Deur Open.* Tram doors close automatically, and they do it quite quickly, so don't hang around.

By Bus: An extensive bus network complements the trams. Many bus routes begin and end at Centraal Station. It's generally faster to go by tram if you have the option, but some points in the city are served only by bus.

By Metro: The Metro can't compare to the labyrinthine systems of Paris, London, and New York, but Amsterdam does have its own Metro, with four lines—50, 51, 53, and 54—that run partly overground and bring people in from the suburbs and home again. You may want to take them simply as a sightseeing excursion, though to be frank, few of the sights on the lines are worth going out of your way for. From Centraal Station, you can use Metro trains to reach both Nieuwmarkt and Waterlooplein in the central zone.

A new Metro line, the Metro Noord/Zuidlijn, is currently under construction to link Amsterdam-Noord (North), under the IJ channel, then south through the center city all the way to Station Zuid/WTC (World Trade Center). It's not due to be completed until 2015.

By Ferry: Free ferries for passengers and two-wheel transportation connect the center city with Amsterdam-Noord (North), across the IJ. The short crossings are free, which makes them ideal micro-cruises for the cash strapped, and they afford fine views of the harbor. Sadly, there's little of interest in Noord, so the free trip may have to be its own attraction. Ferries depart from Waterplein West, a dock on De Ruijterkade behind Centraal Station. One route goes to Buiksloterweg on the north shore, with ferries every 6 to 12 minutes round the clock. A second route goes to IJplein, a more easterly point on the north shore, with ferries every 8 to 15 minutes from 6:30am to around midnight.

By Water Bus: Two different companies operate water buses (rarely, if ever, used by locals) that bring you to, or close to, many of the city's museums, attractions, and shopping and entertainment districts. **Canal Bus** (☎ 020/623-9886; www.canal.nl) has three routes—Green, Red, and Blue—with stops that include Centraal Station, Westermarkt, Leidseplein, Rijksmuseum (with an extension to the RAI Convention Center when big shows are on there), and Waterlooplein. Hours of operation are daily from 10am to 6:30pm, with two buses an hour at peak times. A day pass, valid until noon the next day and including a discount on some museum and attraction admissions, is 18€ for adults, and 12€ for kids ages 4 to 12.

The **Museum Quarter Line** (☎ 020/530-1090; www.lovers.nl) boats transport weary visitors on their pilgrimages from museum to museum and have the added benefit of providing some of the features of a canal-boat cruise. Boats depart from the Rederij Lovers dock in front of Centraal Station daily from 10am to 6:30pm, every 30 minutes in summer, and every 45 minutes in winter. They stop at seven key spots, providing access to museums and other sights. These include the Rijksmuseum, Van Gogh Museum, Stedelijk Museum, Anne Frankhuis, Leidseplein, Vondelpark, Amsterdams Historisch Museum, Flower Market, Museum Het Rembrandthuis, Jewish Historical Museum, Artis Zoo, Muziektheater, Tropenmuseum, and Maritime Museum. A day ticket, valid for 24 hours from the time of purchase, is 19€ for adults, and 15€ for kids ages 4 to 12. Tickets include discounted admission to some museums and attractions.

By Taxi

It used to be that you couldn't simply hail a cab from the street in Amsterdam, but nowadays they often stop if you do. Otherwise, find one of the taxi stands sprinkled around the city, generally near the luxury hotels, at major squares such as the Dam, Spui, Rembrandtplein, Westermarkt, and Leidseplein, and of course at Centraal Station. Taxis have rooftop signs and blue license tags, and are metered.

For a generally reliable service, call **Taxi Centrale Amsterdam (TCA;** ☎ 020/777-7777). TCA's fares begin at 3.10€ when the meter starts and run up at 1.90€ a kilometer, and after 25km (16 miles), 1.40€ a kilometer; waiting time is 31€ per hour. The fare includes a tip, but you may round up or give something for an extra service, like help with your luggage, or for a helpful discourse.

By Water Taxi

Since you're in the city of canals, you might like to splurge on a water taxi. These launches do more or less the same thing as landlubber taxis, except that they do it on the canals and the Amstel River and in the harbor. You can move faster than on land and you get your very own canal cruise. To order one, call **VIP Water-taxi** (☎ 020/535-6363), or pick one up from the dock outside Centraal Station, close to the VVV office. For up to eight people the fare is 60€ for the first 30 minutes, and 40€ for each subsequent half-hour.

By Bike

Instead of renting a car, follow the Dutch example and ride a bicycle. Sunday, when the city is quiet, is a particularly good day to pedal through Vondelpark and along off-the-beaten-path canals, or to practice riding on cobblestones and in bike lanes, crossing bridges, and dodging trams before venturing forth into the fray of an Amsterdam rush hour. There are half a million bikes in the city, so you'll have plenty of company.

Navigating the city on two wheels is mostly safe—or at any rate not as suicidal as it looks—thanks to a vast network of dedicated bike lanes. Bikes even have their own traffic lights. Amsterdam's battle-scarred bike-borne veterans make it almost a point of principle to ignore every safety rule ever written. Though they mostly live to tell the tale, don't think the same will necessarily apply to you.

Bike-rental rates start at 9.50€ a day or 31€ a week; a deposit is required. **Mike's Bike Tours,** Kerkstraat 134 (☎ 020/622-7970; www.mikesbiketoursamsterdam.com; tram: 1, 2, or 5), is a good bet for a rental. So is **MacBike** (☎ 020/620-0985; www.macbike.nl), which rents a range of bikes, including tandems and six-speed touring bikes, and has rental outlets at Centraal Station; Mr. Visserplein 2, close to Waterlooplein (tram: 9 or 14); and Weteringschans 2, off Leidseplein (tram: 1, 2, 5, 7, or 10).

Warning: Always lock both your bike frame and one of the wheels to something solid and fixed, because theft is common.

By Car

Driving in Amsterdam is not recommended. Parking is difficult, traffic is dense, and networks of one-way streets make navigation, even with the best of maps, a problem. You would be much better advised to make use of the city's extensive public transportation or to take cabs.

By Foot

The best way to take in the city is to walk, and the center city is pedestrian-friendly. Carry a good map with you, and watch out for those ubiquitous speeding bikes and speeding trams.

Fast **Facts**

ATMS/CASHPOINTS The easiest and best way to get cash abroad is through an ATM—the **Cirrus** and **Plus** networks span the globe. Most banks charge a fee for international withdrawals—check with your bank before you leave home, and find out your daily limit.

BABYSITTERS A reliable local organization is **Oppascentrale Kriterion** (☎ 020/624-5848), which has vetted babysitters over 18. Its rates are 6€ an hour.

BANKS Most banks are open Monday to Friday from 9am to 4, 5, or 6pm (some stay open Thurs until 7pm). A few are open on Saturday morning. Some shops and most hotels will cash traveler's checks but not at the advantageous rate most banks and foreign exchanges will give you.

BIKE RENTALS See "By Bike," under "Getting Around," above.

BUSINESS HOURS Shops tend to be open from 9:30am to 6pm. Some stay open until 8 or 9pm. Most museums close 1 day a week (often Mon), but may be open some holidays, except Koninginnedag (Queen's Day), Christmas, and New Year's Day.

CONSULATES & EMBASSIES **U.S. Consulate:** Museumplein 19 (☎ 020/575-5309; tram: 3, 5, 12, or 16) **U.K. Consulate:** Koningslaan 44 (☎ 020/676-4343; tram: 2).

Embassies are in The Hague (Den Haag): **U.S. Embassy,** Lange Voorhout 102 (☎ 070/310-2209); **Canadian Embassy,** Sophialaan 7 (☎ 070/311-1600); **U.K. Embassy,** Lange Voorhout 10 (☎ 070/427-0427); **Irish Embassy,** Dr. Kuyperstraat 9 (☎ 070/363-0993); **Australian Embassy,** Carnegielaan 4 (☎ 070/310-8200); **New Zealand Embassy,** Carnegielaan 10 (☎ 070/346-9324).

CREDIT CARDS Credit cards are a safe way to carry money. They also provide a convenient record of all your expenses, and they generally offer good exchange rates. You can withdraw cash advances from your credit cards at banks or ATMs (Cashpoints), provided you know your PIN (call the number on the back of your card if you don't know yours). Keep in mind that when you use your credit card abroad, most banks assess a 2% fee above the 1% fee charged by Visa, MasterCard, and American Express. You also pay interest from the day of your withdrawal, even if you pay your monthly bill on time.

CURRENCY EXCHANGE Cash your traveler's checks at banks or foreign-exchange offices, not at shops or hotels. Most post offices also change traveler's checks or convert money. Currency exchanges are found at Amsterdam's Schiphol Airport and Centraal Station.

CUSTOMS Travelers arriving from a **non–European Union country** can bring in, duty-free, 200 cigarettes (or 250g of tobacco), or 100 cigarillos (or 50 cigars); and 2 liters of wine, or 1 liter of alcohol over 22 proof, or 2 liters under 22 proof; and 50ml of perfume or 0.25 liters of eau de toilette. Customs officials tend to be lenient about general merchandise, realizing the limits are unrealistically low. Travelers arriving from an **E.U. country** can bring any amount of goods into the Netherlands, so long as they are intended for personal use—not for resale; there are generous guideline limits, beyond which the goods may be deemed to be for resale.

DENTISTS See "Emergencies," below.

DOCTORS See "Emergencies," below.

DRUGSTORES In the Netherlands a pharmacy is called an *apotheek* and sells both prescription and nonprescription medicines. Regular open hours are Monday to Saturday from 9am to 6pm. A centrally located pharmacy is **Dam Apotheek,** Damstraat 2 (☎ 020/624-4331; tram: 4, 9, 14, 16, 24, or 25), close to the Nationaal Monument on the Dam. Pharmacies post details of nearby all-night and Sunday pharmacies on their doors.

EMERGENCIES For any emergency (fire, police, ambulance) the number is ☎ 112 from any land line or cellphone. For 24-hour emergency medical or dental service, call the **Central Doctors Service** (☎ 020/592-3434). Residents of an E.U. country must have a European Health Insurance Card to receive full reciprocal health-care benefits in the Netherlands.

EVENT LISTINGS *Amsterdam Day by Day* is published monthly in English and lists all the happenings around town. It's available at any newsstand for 1.95€.

FAMILY TRAVEL **Family Travel** (www.familytravel.com) is an independent, U.S.-based website offering reviews, sightseeing suggestions, and so on.

GAY & LESBIAN TRAVELERS **COC,** Rozenstraat 14 (☎ 020/626-3087; www.cocamsterdam.nl) is the Amsterdam branch of the Dutch lesbian and gay organization. It can answer any questions about anything gay in Holland. The city's largest gay and lesbian bookstore is **Boekhandel Vrolijk,** Paleisstraat 135 (☎ 020/623-5142).

HOLIDAYS National holidays include New Year's Day (Jan 1), Good Friday and Easter Monday (Mar or Apr), Queen's Day (Apr 30), Ascension Day (40 days after Easter), Pentecost Sunday (seventh Sun after Easter) and Pentecost Monday, Christmas Day (Dec 25), and Dec 26.

INSURANCE North Americans with homeowner's or renter's insurance are probably covered for lost luggage. If not, inquire with **Travel Assistance International** (☎ 800/821-2828) or **Travelex** (☎ 800/228-9792), insurers that can also provide trip-cancellation, medical, and emergency evacuation coverage abroad. The website www.moneysupermarket.com compares prices across a wide range of providers for single- and multitrip policies. **For U.K. and Irish citizens,** insurance is always advisable, even if you have a European Health Insurance Card (see "Emergencies," above).

INTERNET ACCESS Many hotels offer Internet access. **The Mad Processor,** Kinkerstraat 11–13 (☎ 020/612-1818; www.madprocessor.com), is open daily from noon until 1 or 2am; access is 2€ an hour.

LIQUOR LAWS Supermarkets, grocery stores, and cafes sell alcoholic beverages. The legal drinking age is 16.

LOST PROPERTY If your luggage is lost, immediately file a lost-luggage claim at the airport, detailing the luggage contents. For most airlines, you must report delayed, damaged, or lost baggage within 4 hours of arrival.

MAIL/POST OFFICES Most post offices in Amsterdam are open Monday through Friday from 9am to 5pm. Stamps can usually be purchased from your hotel reception desk and at larger newsstands, especially ones that sell postcards.

MONEY The currency of the Netherlands is the euro, which can also be used in most other E.U. countries. The exchange rate varies, but at press time, 1 euro was equal to around $1.60 in the United States and 80p in Great Britain. The best way to get cash in Amsterdam is at ATMs or Cashpoints (see above). Credit cards are accepted at almost all hotels, and many shops and restaurants, but you should always have some cash on hand for incidentals and sightseeing admissions.

NEWSPAPERS & MAGAZINES Most kiosks sell English-language newspapers, including the *International Herald Tribune, USA Today,* and British titles such as the *Times* and the *Independent.*

PASSPORTS If your passport is lost or stolen, contact your country's embassy or consulate immediately (see "Consulates & Embassies," above). Before you travel, you should copy the critical pages and keep them separately from your passport.

POLICE Call ☎ 112 for emergencies. The most central police station is at Lijnbaansgracht 219 (☎ 0900/8844; tram: 1, 2, 5, 7, or 10), just off Leidseplein.

SAFETY Be especially aware of child pickpockets. Their method is to get very close to a target, ask for a handout, and deftly help themselves to your money or passport. Robbery at gun- or knifepoint is very rare but not unknown. For more information, consult the U.S. State Department's website at www.travel.state.gov; in the U.K., consult the Foreign Office's website, www.fco.gov.uk; and in Australia, consult the government travel advisory service at www.smartraveller.gov.au.

SENIOR TRAVELERS Mention that you're a senior when you make your travel reservations. As in most cities, people over the age of 60 qualify for reduced admission to Amsterdam theaters, museums, and other attractions, as well as discounted fares on public transport.

SMOKING Smoking is common in Holland, but authorities are clamping down heavily on smoking in public places. It's long been banned in such places as theaters and on public transportation. Since July 1, 2008, smoking has been banned in hotel public spaces, restaurants, cafes, bars, and nightclubs (and other places), except in separate, enclosed smoking rooms where no food or drink is served by the staff.

TAXES Value-added tax, or VAT (BTW in the Netherlands) is 6% to 19%, depending on the amount and product you are purchasing, but non-E.U. visitors can get a refund if they spend 50€ or more in any store that participates in the VAT refund program. The shops will give you a form, which you must get stamped at Customs (allow extra time). Customs may ask to see your purchase, so don't pack it in your checked luggage. Mark the paperwork to request a credit card refund, otherwise you'll be stuck with a check in euros. Another option is to ask for a **Global Refund Form** (☎ 023/524-1909; www.global refund.com) when you make your purchase, and take it to a Global Refund counter at the airport. Your money is refunded on the spot, minus a commission.

TELEPHONES Public phones are found in cafes, post offices, and occasionally on the street. Coin-operated telephones are rare. Most phones take prepaid calling cards, which are available at kiosks, post offices, and currency-exchange stands. They cost 5€, 10€, 20€, or 50€. To make a **direct international call,** first dial 00, then dial the country code, the area code, and the local number. The country code for the **U.S. and Canada** is 1; **Great Britain,** 44; **Ireland,** 353; **Australia,** 61; and **New Zealand,** 64. You can also call the U.S., Canada, the U.K., Ireland, Australia, or New Zealand using **AT&T USA**

Direct, which allows you to avoid hotel surcharges. Call ☎ 0800/022-9111.

For operator assistance, call ☎ 0800/0410.

TICKETS The best outlet is the centrally located Amsterdams Uitburo (AUB) Ticketshop, Leidseplein 26 (☎ 0900/0191; www.amsterdams uitburo.nl). You can buy tickets on their website prior to your arrival. You can also ask your concierge to book tickets for you at the time you book your room.

TIPPING In cafes and restaurants, waiter service is usually included, though you can round the bill up or leave some small change if you like. A service charge is included in taxi fares, but a small tip (1€ to 2€) is always appreciated. If you make the driver wait or are going on a long expensive trip, tip 5%. Tip hotel porters 1€ to 2€ for each piece of luggage.

TOILETS If you use a toilet at a brown cafe or restaurant, it's customary to make some small purchase.

TOURIST OFFICES For tourist information, the best outlets are the official offices of VVV Amsterdam, on platform 2 inside Centraal Station, and at Stationsplein 10 right outside the station, or the agency office in a kiosk facing Stadhouderskade 1 at Leidseplein (all offices ☎ 0900/400-4040).

TOURS The two largest tour companies are **Globus/Cosmos** (☎ 877/245-6287; www.globusandcosmos.com) and **Trafalgar** (☎ 800/854-0103; www.trafalgartours.com). Many major airlines offer air/land package deals that include tours of Amsterdam; ask the airlines or your travel agent for details.

TRAVELERS WITH DISABILITIES Nearly all modern hotels in Amsterdam now have rooms designed for people with disabilities, but many older hotels do not. Not all trams in Amsterdam are fully accessible for wheelchairs, but new trams have low central doors that are accessible. Amsterdam's Metro system is fully accessible.

Amsterdam: **A Brief History**

1200 Fishermen establish a coastal settlement at the mouth of the Amstel River, which is dammed to control periodic flooding; the settlement takes the name "Aemstelledamme."

1300 The bishop of Utrecht grants Amsterdam its first town charter.

1323 Amsterdam's economy receives a boost when it is declared a toll center for beer.

1350 The city becomes a transit point for imported grain, growing in importance as a trade center.

1602 The United East India Company (V.O.C.), destined to become a powerful force in Holland's Golden Age of discovery, exploration, and trade, is founded.

1611 First Amsterdam Stock Exchange opens.

1613 Construction begins on the Herengracht, Keizersgracht, and Prinsengracht canals.

1631 Rembrandt, at age 25, moves to Amsterdam from his native Leiden.

1795 French troops occupy Holland with the aid of Dutch revolutionaries and establish the Batavian Republic; William V flees to England.

1806–10 Louis Bonaparte, Napoleon's brother, reigns as king of Holland.

1813 The Netherlands regains independence from the French.

1910 A flushable water system for the canals is introduced.

1920 Dutch airline KLM launches the world's first scheduled air service, between Amsterdam and London.

1928 The Olympics are held in Amsterdam.

1932 Afsluitdijk (Enclosure Dike) at the head of the Zuider Zee is completed, transforming the sea on which Amsterdam stands into the freshwater IJsselmeer lake.

1940 On May 10 Nazi Germany invades the Netherlands, which surrenders 4 days later.

1944–45 Thousands die during the Hunger Winter, when Nazi occupation forces blockade western Holland.

1945 On May 5 German forces in the Netherlands surrender.

1960S The city takes on the mantle of Europe's hippie capital.

1973 The Van Gogh Museum opens.

1975 Amsterdam's 700th anniversary. Cannabis use is decriminalized.

1987 The *Homomonument,* the world's first public memorial to persecuted gays and lesbians, is unveiled.

2001 The world's first same-sex marriage with a legal status identical to heterosexual matrimony takes place in Amsterdam.

2002 Euro banknotes and coins replace the guilder.

2004 Controversial film director Theo van Gogh is stabbed and shot to death by an Islamist extremist on the streets of Amsterdam.

2006 Homophobic assailants in Amsterdam beat up the editor of the *Washington Blade* gay newspaper.

2008 Smoking in restaurants, cafes, bars, and nightclubs is banned.

Golden Age Art

Although there were earlier prominent Dutch artists, Dutch art really came into its own during the 17th-century Golden Age. Artists were blessed with wealthy patrons whose support allowed them to give free rein to their talents. The primary art patrons were Protestant merchants who commissioned portraits, genre scenes, and still lifes, not the kind of religious works commissioned by the church in Catholic countries. The Dutch were particularly fond of pictures that depicted their world: landscapes, seascapes, domestic scenes, and portraits.

Gerrit van Honthorst
Early 17th-century Utrecht artist **Gerrit van Honthorst** (1590–1656), who had studied in Rome with Caravaggio, brought the new "realism of light and dark," or chiaroscuro, technique to Holland, where he influenced Dutch artists like the young Rembrandt. Honthorst is best

known for lively company scenes such as *The Supper Party* (ca. 1620; Uffizi, Florence), which depicted ordinary people against a plain background and set a style that continued in Dutch art for many years. He often used multiple hidden light sources to heighten the dramatic contrast of lights and darks.

Jacob van Ruisdael

Among the great landscape artists of this period, **Jacob van Ruisdael** (1628–82) stands out. In his paintings, human figures either do not appear at all or are shown almost insignificantly small; vast skies filled with moody clouds often cover two-thirds of the canvas. His *Windmill at Wijk bij Duurstede* (ca.1665; Rijksmuseum, Amsterdam) combines many characteristic elements of his style. The windmill stands in a somber landscape, containing a few small human figures, with a cloud-laden sky and a foreground of agitated water and reeds.

Frans Hals

Antwerp-born **Frans Hals** (ca.1580–1666), the undisputed leader of the Haarlem school (schools differed from city to city), was a great portrait painter whose relaxed, informal, and naturalistic portraits contrast strikingly with the traditional formal masks of Renaissance portraits. His light brushstrokes help convey immediacy and intimacy, making his works perceptive psychological portraits. He had a genius for comic characters, showing men and women as they are and a little less than they are, as in *Malle Babbe* (ca. 1635; Gemäldegalerie, Berlin). As a stage designer of group portraits, Hals's skill is almost unmatched—only Rembrandt is superior. Although he carefully arranged and posed each group, balancing the directions of gesture and glance, his *alla prima* brushwork

(direct laying down of pigment) makes these public images seem spontaneous. It's worth taking a day trip to Haarlem just to visit the Frans Halsmuseum and view such works as his *A Banquet of the Officers of the St. George Civic Guard* (ca.1627) and *Officers and Segeants of the St. Hadrian Civic Guard* (ca. 1633).

Rembrandt

The great genius of the period was **Rembrandt Harmenszoon van Rijn** (1606–69), one of few artists of any period to be known simply by his first name. This painter, whose works hang in places of honor in the world's great museums, may be *the* most famous Amsterdammer, both to outsiders and to today's city residents.

Rembrandt pushed the art of chiaroscuro to unprecedented heights. In his paintings the values of light and dark gradually and softly blend together; this may have diffused some of the drama of chiaroscuro, but it achieved a more truthful appearance. Rembrandt's art seems capable of revealing the soul and inner life of his subjects, and to view his series of 60 self-portraits is to see a remarkable documentation of his own psychological and physical evolution. The etching *Self-Portrait with Saskia* (1636; Rijksmuseum, Amsterdam) shows him with his wife at a prosperous time when he was being commissioned to do portraits of many wealthy merchants. Later self-portraits are more psychologically complex, often depicting a careworn old man whose gaze is nonetheless sharp, compassionate, and wise.

In group portraits like *The Night Watch* (1642) and *The Syndics of the Cloth Guild* (1662), both in the Rijksmuseum, each individual portrait is done with care. The unrivaled harmony of light, color, and movement of these works is a marvel to be appreciated. Compare, too, these robust, masculine works with the tender *The Jewish Bride* (ca. 1665), also in the Rijksmuseum.

In later years Rembrandt was at the height of his artistic powers, but his contemporaries judged his work to be too personal and eccentric. Some considered him a tasteless painter who was obsessed with the ugly and ignorant of color; this opinion prevailed until the 19th century, when Rembrandt's genius was reevaluated.

Jan Vermeer

Perhaps the best known of the "little Dutch masters" who specialized in one genre of painting, such as portraiture, is **Jan Vermeer** (1632–75) of Delft. Although they confined their artistry within a narrow scope, these painters rendered their subjects with an exquisite care and faithfulness to their actual appearances.

Vermeer's work centers on the simple pleasures and activities of domestic life—a woman pouring milk or reading a letter, for example—and all of his simple figures positively glow with color and light. Vermeer placed the figure (usually just one, but sometimes two or more) at the center of his paintings against a background in which

furnishings often provided the horizontal and vertical balance, giving the composition a feeling of stability and serenity. Art historians have determined that Vermeer used mirrors and the camera obscura, an early camera, as compositional aids. A master at lighting interior scenes and rendering true colors, Vermeer was able to create an illusion of three-dimensionality in works such as *The Love Letter* (ca. 1670; Rijksmuseum, Amsterdam). As light—usually afternoon sunshine pouring in from an open window— moves across the picture plane, it caresses and modifies all the colors.

Jan Steen

Born in Leiden, **Jan Steen** (ca. 1626–79) painted marvelous interior scenes, often satirical and didactic in their intent. The allusions on which much of the satire depends may escape most of us today, but any viewer can appreciate the fine drawing, subtle color shading, and warm light that pervades such paintings as *Woman at Her Toilet* (1663) and *The Feast of St. Nicholas* (ca. 1665), both in the Rijksmuseum. Many of his pictures revel in bawdy tavern scenes fueled by overindulgence in beer and gin.

Useful Phrases & Menu Terms

Useful Words & Phrases

ENGLISH	DUTCH	PRONUNCIATION
Hello	Dag/Hallo	*dakh*/ha-*loh*
Good morning	Goedenmorgen	khoo-*yuh*-mor-*khun*
Good afternoon/ evening	Goedenavond	khoo-*yuhn*-af-*ond*
How are you?	Hoe gaat het met U?	*hoo* khaht *et* met *oo?*
Very well	Uitstekend	*out*-stayk-*end*
Thank you	Dank U wel	dahnk *oo wel*
Goodbye	Dag/Tot Ziens	*dakh/tot zeenss*
Good night	Goedenacht	khoo-*duh-nakht*
See you later	Tot straks	*Tot strahkss*

The Savvy Traveler

ENGLISH	DUTCH	PRONUNCIATION
Please	Alstublieft	ahl-*stoo-bleeft*
Yes	Ja	*yah*
No	Neen/nee	*nay*
Excuse me	Pardon	*par*-dawn
Sorry	Sorry	so-*ree*
Do you speak English?	Spreekt U Engels?	*spraykt oo* eng-*els*
Can you help me?	Kunt U mij helpen?	*koont oo* may-*ee* hel-*pen?*
Give me . . .	Geeft U mij . . .	khayft *oo may* . . .
Where is . . . ?	Waar is . . . ?	vahr *iz* . . . ?
the station	het station	*het* stah-*ssyonh*
the post office	het postkantoor	*het* post-*kan-tohr*
a bank	een bank	*ayn* bank
a hotel	een hotel	*ayn* ho-*tel*
a restaurant	een restaurant	*ayn res-to*-rahng
a pharmacy/chemist	een apotheek	*ayn a-po*-tayk
the toilet	het toilet	*het* twah-*let*
To the right	Rechts	*rekhts*
To the left	Links	*links*
Straight ahead	Rechtdoor	*rekht*-doar
I would like . . .	Ik zou graag . . .	*ik zow khrakh* . . .
to eat	eten	ay-*ten*
a room for one night	een kamer voor een nacht	*ayn kah-mer* voor ayn nakht
How much is it?	Hoe veel kost het?	*hoo fayl kawst het*
the check	de rekening	*duh* ray-*ken-ing*
When?	Wanneer?	*vah*-neer
yesterday	gisteren	khis-*ter-en*
today	vandaag	*van*-dahkh
tomorrow	morgen	mor-*khen*
breakfast	ontbijt	ohnt-*bayt*
lunch	lunch	*lunch*
dinner	diner	dee-*nay*

Numbers

ENGLISH	DUTCH	PRONUNCIATION
one	een	*ayn*
two	twee	*tway*
three	drie	*dree*
four	vier	*veer*
five	vijf	*vayf*
six	zes	*zes*
seven	zeven	zay-*vun*
eight	acht	*akht*
nine	negen	nay-*khen*
ten	tien	*teen*
eleven	elf	*elf*
twelve	twaalf	*tvahlf*
thirteen	dertien	dayr-*teen*
fourteen	veertien	vayr-*teen*
fifteen	vijftien	vayf-*teen*

ENGLISH	DUTCH	PRONUNCIATION
sixteen	zestien	zes-*teen*
seventeen	zeventien	zay-*vun-teen*
eighteen	achttien	akh-*teen*
nineteen	negentien	nay-*khun-teen*
twenty	twintig	twin-*tikh*

Days of the Week

ENGLISH	DUTCH	PRONUNCIATION
Monday	Maandag	mahn-*dakh*
Tuesday	Dinsdag	deens-*dakh*
Wednesday	Woensdag	voohns-*dakh*
Thursday	Donderdag	donder-*dakh*
Friday	Vrijdag	vray-*dakh*
Saturday	Zaterdag	zahter-*dakh*
Sunday	Zondag	zohn-*dakh*

Months

ENGLISH	DUTCH	PRONUNCIATION
January	Januari	yahn-*oo-aree*
February	Februari	fayhb-*roo-aree*
March	Maart	*mahrt*
April	April	*ah*-pril
May	Mai	mah-*eey*
June	Juni	*yoo*-nee
July	Juli	*yoo*-lee
August	August	*awh*-khoost
September	September	*sep*-tem-*buhr*
October	Oktober	*oct*-oah-*buhr*
November	November	*noa*-vem-*buhr*
December	December	*day*-sem-*buhr*

Dutch Menu Savvy

BASICS

DUTCH	ENGLISH
ontbijt	breakfast
lunch	lunch
diner	dinner
voorgerechten	starters
hoofdgerechten	main courses
nagerechten	desserts
boter	butter
boterham	sandwich
brood	bread
stokbrood	French bread
honing	honey
hutspot	mashed potatoes and carrots
jam	jam
kaas	cheese
mosterd	mustard
pannekoeken	pancakes

DUTCH	ENGLISH
peper	pepper
saus	sauce
suiker	sugar
zout	salt

SOUPS *(SOEPEN)*

DUTCH	ENGLISH
aardappelsoep	potato soup
bonensoep	bean soup
erwtensoep	pea soup (usually includes bacon or sausage)
groentensoep	vegetable soup
kippensoep	chicken soup
soep	soup
tomatensoep	tomato soup
uiensoep	onion soup

EGGS *(EIER)*

DUTCH	ENGLISH
eieren	eggs
hardgekookte eieren	hard-boiled eggs
zachtgekookte eieren	soft-boiled eggs
omelette	omelet
roereieren	scrambled eggs
spiegeleieren	fried eggs
uitsmijter	fried eggs and ham on bread

FISH *(VIS)*

DUTCH	ENGLISH
forel	trout
garnalen	prawns
gerookte zalm	smoked salmon
haring	herring
kabeljauw	cod
kreeft	lobster
makreel	mackerel
mosselen	mussels
oesters	oysters
paling	eel
sardienen	sardines
schelvis	haddock
schol	plaice
tong	sole
zalm	salmon

MEATS *(VLEES)*

DUTCH	ENGLISH
bief	beef
biefstuk	steak
eend	duck
fricandeau	roast pork
gans	goose
gehakt	minced meat
haasbiefstuk	filet steak

ham	ham
kalfsvlees	veal
kalkoen	turkey
kip	chicken
konijn	rabbit
koude schotel	cold cuts
lamscotelet	lamb chops
lamsvlees	lamb
lever	liver
ragout	beef stew
rookvlees	smoked meat
runder	beef
spek	bacon
worst	sausage

VEGETABLES & SALADS (GROENTEN/SLA)

DUTCH	ENGLISH
aardappelen	potatoes
asperges	asparagus
augurken	pickles
bieten	beets
bloemkool	cauliflower
bonen	beans
champignons	mushrooms
erwten	peas
groenten	vegetables
knoflook	garlic
komkommer	cucumber
komkommersla	cucumber salad
kool	cabbage
patates frites	french fries
prei	leek
prinsesseboonen	green beans
purée	mashed potatoes
radijsen	radishes
rapen	turnips
rijst	rice
sla	lettuce, salad
spinazie	spinach
tomaten	tomatoes
uien	onions
wortelen	carrots
zuurkool	sauerkraut

DESSERTS (NAGERECHTEN)

DUTCH	ENGLISH
appelgebak	apple pie
appelmoes	applesauce
cake	cake
compòte	stewed fruits
gebak	pastry
ijs	ice cream

DUTCH	ENGLISH
jonge kaas	young cheese (mild)
koekjes	cookies
oliebollen	doughnuts
oude kaas	old cheese (strong)
room	cream
slagroom	whipped cream
smeerkaas	cheese spread
speculaas	spiced cookies

FRUITS *(VRUCHTEN)*

DUTCH	ENGLISH
aapel	apple
aardbei	strawberry
ananas	pineapple
citroen	lemon
druiven	grapes
framboos	raspberry
kersen	cherries
peer	pear
perzik	peach
pruimen	plums

BEVERAGES *(DRANKEN)*

DUTCH	ENGLISH
bier (or pils)	beer
cognac	brandy
fles	bottle
glas	glass
jenever	gin
koffie	coffee
melk	milk
rode wijn	red wine
thee	tea
water	water
mineraal water	sparkling water
witte wijn	white wine

COOKING TERMS

DUTCH	ENGLISH
gebakken	fried
gebraden	roast
gegrild	grilled
gekookt	boiled/cooked
gerookt	smoked
geroosteerd	boiled
gestoofd	stewed
goed doorbakken	well done
half doorbakken	medium
koud	cold
niet doorbakken	rare
warm	hot

Toll-Free Numbers & Websites

AER LINGUS
☎ *800/474-7424 in the U.S.*
☎ *0818/365-000 in Ireland*
www.aerlingus.com

AIR CANADA
☎ *888/247-2262 in the U.S. and Canada*
www.aircanada.com

AIR FRANCE
☎ *800/237-2747 in the U.S.*
☎ *800/667-2747 in Canada*
☎ *3654 in France*
www.airfrance.com

AIR NEW ZEALAND
☎ *800/262-1234 in the U.S.*
☎ *800/663-5494 in Canada*
☎ *0800/737-000 in New Zealand*
www.airnewzealand.com

ALITALIA
☎ *800/223-5730 in the U.S.*
☎ *800/361-8366 in Canada*
☎ *06-2222 in Italy*
www.alitalia.com

AMERICAN AIRLINES
☎ *800/433-7300 in the U.S. and Canada*
www.aa.com

AUSTRIAN AIRLINES
☎ *800/843-0002 in the U.S. and Canada*
☎ *05/1766-1000 in Austria*
www.aua.com

BMI
☎ *800/788-0555 in the U.S.*
☎ *0870/607-0555 in Britain*
www.flybmi.com

BRITISH AIRWAYS
☎ *800/247-9297 in the U.S. and Canada*
☎ *0844/493-0787 in Britain*
www.britishairways.com

CONTINENTAL AIRLINES
☎ *800/231-0856 in the U.S. and Canada*
www.continental.com

DELTA AIR LINES
☎ *800/241-4141 in the U.S. and Canada*
www.delta.com

EASYJET
No U.S. number
☎ *0905/821-0905 in the U.K.*
www.easyjet.com

IBERIA
☎ *800/772-4642 in the U.S. and Canada*
☎ *902/400-500 in Spain*
www.iberia.com

ICELANDAIR
☎ *800/223-5500 in the U.S. and Canada*
☎ *354/50-50-700 in Iceland*
www.icelandair.com

KLM
☎ *800/225-2525 in the U.S. and Canada*
☎ *020/474-7747 in the Netherlands*
www.klm.com

LUFTHANSA
☎ *800/645-3880 in the U.S.*
☎ *800/563-5954 in Canada*
☎ *0180/583-8426 in Germany*
www.lufthansa.com

NORTHWEST AIRLINES
☎ *800/225-2525 in the U.S. and Canada*
www.nwa.com

QANTAS
☎ *800/227-4500 in the U.S. and Canada*
☎ *131313 in Australia*
www.qantas.com

SCANDINAVIAN AIRLINES
☎ *800/221-2350 in the U.S. and Canada*
☎ *7010-2000 in Denmark*
☎ *05400 in Norway*
☎ *0070/727-727 in Sweden*
www.flysas.com

SOUTH AFRICAN AIRLINES
☎ *800/722-9675 in the U.S. and Canada*
☎ *0861/359-722 in South Africa*
www.flysaa.com

SWISS INTERNATIONAL AIR LINES
☎ *877/359-7947 in the U.S. and Canada*
☎ *0848/700-700 in Switzerland*
www.swiss.com

UNITED AIRLINES
☎ *800/538-2929 in the U.S. and Canada*
www.united.com

US AIRWAYS
☎ *800/622-1015 in the U.S. and Canada*
www.usairways.com

VIRGIN ATLANTIC AIRWAYS
☎ *800/821-5438 in the U.S. and Canada*
☎ *0870/380-2007 in the U.K.*
www.virgin-atlantic.com

Index

See also Accommodations and Restaurant indexes, below.

Photo **Credits**

p viii: © Jon Arnold/AGE Fotostock; p 3 bottom: © Richard Nebesky/Lonely Planet Images;
p 3 middle: © Art Resource, NY; p 4 top: © Art Kowalsky/Alamy; p 4 bottom: © Barbara
Opitz/Bildarchiv Mannheim GmbH/Alamy; p 5: © Jon Arnold/AGE Fotostock; p 7 bottom:
© Ken Welsh/AGE Fotostock; p 8 top: © Bill Heinsohn/Alamy; p 9 bottom: © Sergio Pitzmitz/
AGE Fotostock; p 11 middle: © Ken Welsh/Alamy; p 12 top: © Richard Nebesky/Lonely
Planet Images; p 12 bottom: © Javier Larrea/AGE Fotostock; p 13 top: © Juan José Pascual/
AGE Fotostock; p 13 bottom: © Richard Nebesky/Lonely Planet Images; p 14 bottom:
© Graham Salter/Lebrecht Music and Arts Photo Library/Alamy; p 15 top: © Vittorio Sciosia/
Alamy; p 17 top: © Courtesy Museum Willet@@hyHolthuysen; p 18 top: © Brian Lawrence/
SuperStock; p 18 bottom: © Martin Moos/Lonely Planet Images; p 19 top: © Peter Phipp/
AGE Fotostock; p 20 top: © Walter Bibikow/Jon Arnold Images/Alamy; p 21: © Bridgeman
Art Library; p 23 bottom: © Kim Zwarts/Cobra Museum; p 24 top: © Courtesy Hermitage
Amsterdam; p 25 bottom: © Jochen Tack/Alamy; p 28 bottom: © Alberto Paredes/
AGE Fotostock; p 29 bottom: © Sergio Pitzmitz/AGE Fotostock; p 30 top: © Richard Nebesky/
Lonely Planet Images; p 30 bottom: © Robert Hart Photography/Lloyd Hotel; p 34 bottom:
© Courtesy Artis Amsterdam Zoo; p 35 top: © Popperfoto/Alamy; p 36 top: © Sergio
Pitzmitz/Alamy; p 36 bottom: © Martin Moos/Lonely Planet Images; p 40 top: © Martin
Moos/Lonely Planet Images; p 40 bottom: © Art Kowalsky/Alamy; p 41 top: © Courtesy
Houseboat Museum; p 44 bottom: © The Cover Story/Corbis; p 45 top: © Horacio Villalo-
bos/Corbis; p 45 bottom: © David Crausby/Alamy; p 46 top: © culliganphoto/Alamy; p 46
bottom: © Avatra Images/Alamy; p 47: © SIME s.a.s./eStock Photo; p 49 bottom: © Florian
Monheim/Bildarchiv Monheim GmbH/Alamy; p 50 bottom: © Dave Bartruff/Index Stock
Imagery; p 51 bottom: © Courtesy Museum Van Loon; p 53 bottom: © Martin Moos/Lonely
Planet Images; p 54 bottom: © SIME s.a.s./eStock Photo; p 54 top: © SIME s.a.s./eStock
Photo; p 55 top: © DK Images/Index Stock Imagery; p 57 bottom: © Ken Welsh/Alamy; p 58
top: © Adam Woolfitt/Corbis; p 59 top: © Richard Nebesky/Lonely Planet Images; p 61 bot-
tom: © P. Munoz/eStock Photo; p 62 top: © Walter Bibikow/Folio Inc./Alamy; p 62 bottom:
© Florian Monheim/Bildarchiv Monheim GmbH/Alamy; p 63 top: © Sergio Pitzmitz/AGE
Fotostock; p 64 middle: © David Crausby/Alamy; p 65: © Christian Sarramon/Corbis; p 66
bottom: © DK Images/Index Stock Imagery; p 70 middle: © V&A Images/Alamy; p 70 bottom: © Bridgeman Art Library; p 71 top: © Atlantide S.N.C./AGE Fotostock; p 71 bottom:
© Duncan Johnson/Cephas Picture Library/Alamy; p 72 middle: © Powered by Light/Alan
Spencer/Alamy; p 72 bottom: © Ken Welsh/Alamy; p 73 top: © Helene Rogers/Alamy; p 73
bottom: © Martin Moos/Lonely Planet Images; p 74 top: © Neal Lankester/Alamy; p 75 bot-
tom: © Comstock Images/Alamy; p 76 bottom: © Martin Moos/Lonely Planet Images; p 77:
© Kindra Clineff/Index Stock Imagery; p 79 bottom: © eye35.com/Alamy; p 80 top: © Peter
Phipp/AGE Fotostock; p 81 bottom: © Benelux Press/Index Stock Imagery; p 83 bottom:
© Hill Creek Pictures/Index Stock Imagery; p 84 top: © John Lawrence/Getty Images; p 84
bottom: © Jon Arnold/AGE Fotostock; p 85 top: © Christian Sarramon/Corbis; p 87 middle:
© Art Kowalsky/Alamy; p 87 bottom: © Peter Phipp/AGE Fotostock; p 88 top: © B. Tanaka/
Getty Images; p 89: © Richard Nebesky/Lonely Planet Images; p 90 bottom: © Richard
Nebesky/Lonely Planet Images; p 94 bottom: © Atlantide S.N.C./AGE Fotostock; p 95 top:
© David Hanson/Getty Images; p 96 top: © Courtesy The Dylan Amsterdam; p 97 bottom:

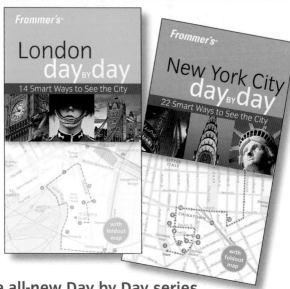